HOW TO GET A MORTGAGE IN 24 HOURS

HOW TO GET A MORTGAGE IN 24 HOURS

Third Edition

JAMES E. A. LUMLEY

JOHN WILEY & SONS, INC.

New York ▪ Chichester ▪ Brisbane ▪ Toronto ▪ Singapore

Library of Congress Cataloging in Publication Data:

Lumley, James E. A.
   How to get a mortgage in 24 hours / by James E. A. Lumley. — 3rd
ed.
     p. cm.
   Includes bibliographical references.
   ISBN 0-471-59937-9 (cloth). — ISBN 0-471-59938-7 (paper)
   1. Mortgage loans—United States. I. Title.
   HG2040.5. U5L85   1994
   332.7'2—dc20   93-26682

To
Briana Rose Lumley

PREFACE

The Third Edition of *How to Get a Mortgage in 24 Hours* continues to help you find low-cost financing in the quickest possible time. It explores many alternative mortgage plans and offers new guidelines to help you choose among competing options, all with the goal of saving you money. I have also included thorough discussions of how loans work, what they cost, and how to choose what is superior for you.

Two chapters have been added to this edition. The first explains the process of prequalifying yourself with a lender before you find a specific property. The second covers the various aspects of trading up to a more spacious and more expensive home or downsizing to more modest quarters.

In recent years, we have become a nation of movers. Each year, residential transfers increase almost 10% over the previous year. One reason is the moderate interest rates that are currently available on property loans. As rates fall, it becomes easier to sell one house to buy another. Today, mortgage rates are lower than they were on properties financed at any time in the 1980s. The future bodes well for the sustaining of these modest rates as well as for the availability of large quantities of mortgage money.

Theoretically, all we need to do to get this money is to ask. Although, to some extent, this is true, the process is not as easy as it sounds. Banks have so many requests for mortgage money that they often apply arbitrary and selective standards in determining to whom they will lend these funds. Also, time can be crucial in securing a mortgage commitment. In this book, you will find shortcuts through this selection process. Further, whether you get your financing from a banker or a seller, these methods will guide you in getting a mortgage in the quickest time.

Is it possible to get a mortgage in 24 hours? Yes—if you are willing to spend time and energy beforehand targeting that one-day commitment. This means you will have to choose your lender with care and prepare a convincing presentation of your case. And, you will have to make allowances ahead of time for certain procedures beyond your control.

What are some of the procedures that can delay a mortgage commitment? The limited or overloaded regularly scheduled meetings of a bank's mortgage committee is often a slow-down point. A second bottleneck is the current shortage of state-certified appraisers. In these busy buying times—in addition to complying with new federal regulations—lenders may have to wait several weeks for appraisals to be completed. The present shortage of real estate attorneys causes still another delay. And a fourth obstruction has been the backlog of credit reports. A few years ago, a bank could expect a credit check to take one to three days. Currently, that same report may take more than a month.

As a home buyer who wants a mortgage and wants it now, you must expect delays. You can circumvent time by doing much of the legwork, planning, and information gathering ahead of time. This book will tell you how to go about those tasks and thus speed up the lending process.

In your quest for a quick mortgage, you will find lenders willing to help. Many banks are growing increasingly aggressive in their pursuit of reliable borrowers. The current competition among lenders has forced them to be responsive to the needs of consumers by processing loans more quickly.

Some large banks are even promising homebuyers mortgage commitments within minutes. These near-instant loan commitments require only pertinent information about you and the property. And, like all loans secured by real estate, they require an appraisal, which may be done that day.

Many banks (inevitably the one that offers you the lowest interest rate) cannot offer sudden cheer even though, to remain competitive, they have speeded up their paperwork in recent years. The key is information; it takes the correct facts—particularly employment proof and an appraisal—for the bank to act quickly.

However, for every obstacle that hinders a rapid response, new techniques lead the way to faster approval. Specifically, computer technology that can cut through paperwork is, in many banks, shortening evaluation time. In fact, your job is to hustle up the necessary paperwork. Your purpose is to show the lender you qualify for the mortgage—and should get it "now."

Often, you can help assure yourself of a mortgage even before you choose a property by prequalifying yourself for a loan, a procedure described in the new chapter on prequalification. Next, for quick service after you find the home you want, you must satisfy the lender on three basic points: first, the property's value, second, your ability to repay, and third, the worth for the lender.

You will learn how to make a mortgage proposal that satisfies the lender on these points. Professional investors have used such proposals for years. Now you can use one to bypass or speed up the bank's appraisal and credit processes. The proposal is easy to prepare. It requires only a few pages to show your banker you are a sound, rational borrower who understands the financial aspects of a mortgage and the bank's need for profit. It convinces the lender that you are familiar with the loan process and—more important—that you are a good risk for a loan.

Although loan conditions vary in each area of the United States, my instructions for writing a proposal and accompanying advice for negotiating interest rate and terms will help you get your mortgage funds quickly. This information can also save you thousands of dollars. The proposal is an excellent means to assure your getting the best deal for the money you need.

Unlike other books on mortgages, this volume is not a technical rendition on financial or accounting techniques. In fact, only a few charts show how the basic mortgage works. Instead, I have provided a thorough discussion of the many mortgages available and a description of strategies for negotiating the prize mortgage in the shortest amount of time, at the lowest possible cost. These facts will not make you a financial wizard. After reading this book, however, you will be able to walk into a bank and talk to a mortgage officer on equal terms.

I am not a banker; my experience has been gained working as a real estate broker. Nevertheless, buying and financing my own investment property have given me insight into getting a rapid and favorable commitment on a mortgage.

This book is easy to understand, even when it explains a specific problem such as loan payoff or term negotiation. It gives you step-by-step, surefire methods to achieve success.

The following text explains how the different types of mortgages work—from conventional loans to adjustable-rate mortgages to creative financing with sellers. In providing the information you need to make intelligent decisions, it doesn't assume you have any experience with banks or mortgages. Instead, it leads you through the basics of what mortgages are all about, how they work, and how to select the right one.

The information in each chapter can stand alone, without reference to previously presented information. If you are familiar with conventional mortgages, you can skip that chapter and proceed to the chapter on seller financing. Or perhaps you want to compare conventional and adjustable rate loans, so you skip the explanations of how each kind of loan works.

The material in this book will challenge you by making you think about the different ways to construct a mortgage with either a bank or a seller. Further it will tell you what terms can benefit you most.

Be wary of the many different formats offered by lending institutions. Practically all mortgage choices are variants of the basic fixed rate conventional loan or the adjustable mortgage. It is still a complex transaction, but with wise comparison shopping you will find the right mortgage, no matter what type.

In Chapter 1, you will learn how to construct a mortgage proposal for financing any property in any market in the quickest amount of time. Chapter 2, new to the Third Edition, shows how to prequalify for a mortgage before finding the actual property. Chapter 3 explains the common types of mortgages. Chapter 4 helps you decide how much money you can comfortably afford to borrow, and Chapter 5 shows you how to choose from the variety of loan formats available.

Chapter 6 gives many sources for mortgage money and explains how to approach each one. Chapter 7 explains conventional financing and how to negotiate the lowest possible interest rate and most helpful terms. In Chapter 8, I discuss the advantages and disadvantages of adjustable rate mortgages, as well as how to negotiate them and how to protect yourself against pitfalls. Chapter 9 explores the many aspects of creative financing that you can negotiate with sellers.

In Chapter 10, you will learn about getting a mortgage when you have little or no cash to put down. Chapter 11 gives you inside information on many additional techniques for financing a property, and Chapter 12 discusses home equity loans including how they can help tap your present equity. Chapter 13, on refinancing, shows you how to get cash or combine existing loans, while Chapter 14, also new to this edition, explains how to use today's low interest rates to trade up or down.

The focus of this book is not on how to make millions in the real estate business. To be sure, you may make a fortune—real estate has the potential to appreciate over the long term. Further, since the interest you pay on a mortgage is tax deductible, borrowing money to buy real estate is a superior privilege. The following pages will show you how to negotiate the most advantageous mortgage at the fairest cost and terms, and get the lender's commitment in the shortest possible time.

You will want to heed carefully the many "Key Points" and "Caution Notes" throughout the book. Key Points are basic truths—the do's of getting a mortgage. They offer positive solutions. Caution Notes are the dont's; they point out obvious, and sometimes not so obvious, procedures to avoid.

Pay attention to both the problems and the solutions. With honesty and perseverance, you will get the right mortgage in the shortest amount of time, assuring your financial success in real estate.

JAMES E. A. LUMLEY

Amherst, Massachusetts

CONTENTS

9. WHEN THE SELLER GIVES YOU THE MORTGAGE

10. WHAT TO DO WHEN YOU HAVE LITTLE OR NO CASH TO PUT DOWN

11. INNOVATIVE TECHNIQUES FOR CREATIVE FINANCING — 185

12. HOME EQUITY LOANS — 209

13. REFINANCING YOUR EXISTING LOAN — 225

HOW TO GET
A MORTGAGE
IN 24 HOURS

HOW TO GET YOUR MORTGAGE IN 24 HOURS 1

THE MAGIC OF BORROWING OTHER PEOPLE'S MONEY

In the not-too-distant past, buyers seeking real estate believed it was preferable to buy property with all cash. In fact, many people had this attitude into the 1960s. A dramatic turnabout began in the early 1970s when the annual inflation rate edged higher than 4%, then a dreadfully high figure. The value of money dropped accordingly. Paying all cash became an imprudent way to purchase a property. As inflation spiraled in the 1980s, we continued to believe it would be downright foolish not to get a mortgage when buying real estate. Today, with less inflation, we still seek a mortgage to increase our capital.

However, getting a mortgage has been popular longer than just the past few decades. Our parents and often our grandparents, had financial help, though minimal by our standards, in the form of a mortgage when they bought real estate.

■ *KEY POINT: Some form of mortgage financing has always been available.*

In the past century, millions of people have found security in buying a home or investment property. They do this by using other people's money in the form of a mortgage. Today, some buyers consider it smart to put down little of their own money

1

or no cash at all although full financing is not always desirable in purchasing property. When an owner has little equity in a property and thereby can easily walk away, the bank may be less likely to grant a loan. And, even if an owner incurs difficulty in meeting payments, banks never want to foreclose.

Consider what a mortgage is. Whether given by a bank, the former owner of a property, or even a third party, a mortgage is a legal, secured instrument on a piece of real estate. It is a negotiation of an amount of money, from either a bank or a private party, that will be paid back in regular installments by the new borrower of the money.

■ *KEY POINT: A mortgage is a negotiated loan secured by a property and paid back in installments.*

Where does this money come from? The most popular source of money in investment property in the United States is a mortgage bank or thrift. A mortgage bank, savings and loan (as a thrift is known), or some other government-insured institution is legally chartered to dispense funds to buyers of property. It, in turn, holds a secured instrument in that property until said mortgage is paid in full.

Now, an important fact about mortgages. Are they based on the bank's money? No, frequently not. The money lent to the borrower is often money that is either in the bank due to savings-account deposits, or, it is borrowed outright from other larger banks, which in turn get their funds from savings, investors, and other sources.

■ *KEY POINT: Banks lend other people's money.*

What is the mortgage bank's motivation in doing this? The bank gains its pool of funds from its depositors. For example, these small investors invest small amounts of money, perhaps at a 3% to 5% rate of return. The bank, in turn, takes this conglomeration of funds and re-invests it in the form of mortgages. It could be lent at rates ranging anywhere between 4 and 9%, depending on the type of loan.

Though these rates are at a historical low, banks still make a lot of money in mortgage interest. In this book, you will find many tactics for negotiating to get the most worthwhile mortgage and lowest interest rate.

■ *CAUTION NOTE: Banks make considerable money on interest they charge you.*

If you are buying a house or an investment property, a mortgage is probably a critical need for you. The major object in finding and making the deal, even more vital than the property itself, is how you will finance it. There are many choices. The mortgage bank, as we have mentioned, is one. The other type of mortgage is from a seller. New and interesting techniques to borrow from a bank or seller are discussed in the following chapters.

■ *KEY POINT: Choosing among available financing is the biggest decision in buying.*

Today's historically low rates have touched off a boom in home mortgage financing as well as in refinancing existing mortgages, which often involves converting an adjustable-rate mortgage to a fixed-rate loan. Banks, as well as thrifts, have responded with a wave of advertising and marketing campaigns as they try to wrest the business from each other.

Not only are banks trying to keep their existing customers from refinancing at other lenders, they are trying to lure new borrowers. This competition is likely to stimulate increasingly higher levels of mortgage activity. For borrowers, this reaching out for business by lenders is a splendid boon. With many banks seeking new customers, the decision to grant a loan is often rapid and positive.

■ *KEY POINT: Low interest rates have spurred banks to compete for customers.*

Often your home is a superior investment. Surprising increases in value over short periods, sometimes only a few years, have historically made home purchases outstanding investments. Although it is also true that values have decreased in many areas of the country, over time even these investments have edged up.

You also may wish to purchase a summer or vacation home. Here again, the use of borrowed money can make you rich. In investment real estate, the financing you arrange is critical in determining how much money you will make. So, here, we will learn how to negotiate the right amount and type of financing.

■ *KEY POINT:* *Borrowing money is the key to becoming rich.*

Real estate, then, is a business of borrowing money. It is the use of *other people's money* (OPM) to secure a tangible asset—real estate. Whether lived in by you or rented out, it will grow in value. Also, you may enjoy large tax savings.

■ *KEY POINT:* *Real estate is a vehicle for borrowing money.*

Other people's money is the magic we use to assure our own financial security. The mortgage allows you to finance the house you live in or an income-producing building and to pay back this loan from money you earn from your regular employment. Or, you may pay it out of the rental income from the investment itself. The mortgage allows you to get ownership of expensive property by putting down only a fraction of cash on the total purchase price.

■ *KEY POINT:* *A mortgage allows you to make a larger purchase than would be possible if you had to pay the total price in cash.*

Discussed here are ways to borrow as much money as you need with a minimum down payment. The use of other people's money can often be the key to home ownership and investment success.

THE TRUTH ABOUT MONEY LENDERS

Mortgage lenders never, never want to foreclose. Once they have lent money, it is extremely important to them that they have made the right decision. Never, except under the worst of circumstances, do they want to take back the property. This is true even if payments are not being made on the loan, and it unfolds that the loan might be in default.

During the recession in the early 1990s, the loss of jobs has created an upswing in the number of home mortgage loans that are past due or on the verge of foreclosure. As astounding as it seems to many homeowners, however, lenders prefer to work out a deal rather than foreclose. Lenders make money on interest. If the payment schedule is renegotiated to make it easier on the homeowner, money (interest) still goes to the lender. For lenders, foreclosures—from attorneys' fees to the loss of interest income—only cost money.

■ *KEY POINT: Lenders never want to foreclose.*

The lender is always open to the chance of extended payments, refinancing, or almost anything that will avoid the decision to foreclose. Foreclosure to them means that they have failed. They have neglected to realize the problems inherent in that particular loan. They are in the business of lending money, which in turn makes them a profit. They are not in the business of managing property, particularly property that must be resold. For an institution, this process is often difficult and time consuming.

■ *KEY POINT: Banks almost always allow refinancing or extended payments.*

When you're seeking a mortgage, money is a strong motivation for lenders; they want to make a profit. This leads us to the most important desire of mortgage lenders. They want to loan you money. They must lend you money. In their minds, as long as you can satisfy certain minimum financial requirements, they will quickly agree to loan you money.

■ *KEY POINT:* *Lenders exist to lend you money.*

You may have heard of friends who dealt with a standoffish mortgage officer who pushed them aside with a complicated rigmarole of paperwork that made the process exasperating. This may have even happened to you.

■ *CAUTION NOTE:* *Banks and paperwork inhibit the loan process.*

Nevertheless, if you're suffering from a financial problem, a lender can be your bosom friend. Many lenders realize the unfortunate circumstances that have befallen many of their borrowers and are willing to renegotiate the terms of home loans. Your lender may agree to temporarily lower your loan's interest rate or to stretch out your payments over a longer period. Either option will effectively reduce your monthly housing bill. Alternatively, the lender might let you make "interest-only" payments until your employment situation improves.

■ *KEY POINT:* *Lenders will help when you're in trouble.*

The secret to getting a mortgage is to understand that the banks must lend out their money. If they don't lend it to you and other borrowers, they cannot produce the profits to pay back their depositors or those from whom they have borrowed the money now being requested by you.

In this book, you will find guidelines that describe how you can meet the requirements for getting mortgage money in the shortest amount of time.

THE QUICKEST WAY TO GET MORTGAGE FINANCING FOR A HOME OR SMALL INVESTMENT

Time is usually of the essence in getting a mortgage loan. Without the right information, however, many lenders are unable to handle applications with dispatch. This can stretch processing time from weeks to months. Today's lower interest rates, which are generating more loan demand as well as sharper screening processes, have exacerbated this problem. Lenders insist, however, that the longest delays occur when borrowers provide incomplete information. In this book, we address how to reduce such delays.

■ *CAUTION NOTE: Financing delays are often the result of submitting incomplete information.*

Shopping on your own or with your local real estate agent, you may have found the house you want. You may have even agreed with the seller on price and have signed a purchase agreement. In fact, most lenders will not start processing an application until a borrower submits a signed sales contract. Lenders, however, do look favorably on your prequalifying for a loan before you settle on a property. Prequalifying means you check out what a bank requires before looking for a home. We will deal with this procedure in the next chapter.

■ *CAUTION NOTE: Application processing usually requires a signed purchase agreement with a seller.*

■ *KEY POINT: Prequalifying for a loan speeds the process.*

You may have agreed to take over the property in so many days if you meet certain conditions, such as obtaining financing from a local lending institution. Typically, though you may not be taking over the property for another month or longer, you are given a limited amount of time—usually 5 to 10 days—in which to secure from a mortgage lender a commitment that you will get mortgage funds when the deed passes from seller to buyer.

■ *KEY POINT: Sales are often conditional on financing.*

In this "deposit-taken" stage of a pending sale, real estate brokers often don't take the property off the market. Even if you have arranged to purchase a house at full price and have signed a purchase agreement with the seller, the property is held by the brokers in a state of limbo. It means the potential sale to you could fall through should there be any problems with financing. Usually, there are none, but brokers may still show your intended property, explaining to a second buyer that you, the first buyer, have the right of first refusal because your sale is conditional on financing.

■ *CAUTION NOTE: Sales can fall through without a speedy financing commitment.*

This need not be a worrisome problem. Usually, financing is approved for the first buyer, and the sale goes through. However, it is critical for you to assure there are no slipups in your getting a mortgage commitment. The question then becomes "What is the quickest way to arrange financing?" The answer is simply this: All mortgage lenders have a short list of principles that you must satisfy before they give out any mortgage money.

■ *CAUTION NOTE: Bank rules must be satisfied before loan approval.*

These questions are forthright. You will see they're easy to solve with a little preliminary work. Here we will take the mystery out of getting a mortgage in the shortest amount of time. You can get a mortgage in 24 hours—approval on your loan request the day after your initial presentation to the bank. This is not unusual. Real estate brokers and developers, as well as those who have mortgages, do this all the time.

■ *KEY POINT: Commitments on a loan often are gained in one day.*

What you are going to learn here is some of their time-tested secrets for getting such a commitment; specifically, what you need to do to get a loan. Right now, it may seem to be a mystery. It is not. By no means can a mortgage be secured by an easy trick. But, by following several simple procedures, you can assure that 99% of the time you will get the mortgage of your choice in 24 hours.

■ *KEY POINT: Getting a loan in 24 hours is not a mystery.*

Often, for technical reasons, it might take several days for a particular bank to consider your loan application. Some loan committees in small banks do not meet daily. Even in this situation—if you have done your homework—the bank's loan officer may assure you that you have met the bank's criteria. In big banks that have large pools of mortgage funds to lend out, mortgage decisions are frequently made daily; all you need is to be prepared with the information required by the bank in making its decision.

■ *KEY POINT: Preparation is the key to getting a favorable mortgage commitment quickly.*

HOW TO SATISFY A LENDER IN THREE EASY STEPS: VALUE/QUALITY OF A PROPERTY; SOURCE OF MONEY TO REPAY THE LOAN; PROFITABILITY FOR THE LENDER

When lenders make loans, they make three important decisions. The first involves the quality of the property: Is the property worth what you have agreed to pay to the seller? This should not be a problem. Presumably you are buying property in the open market, probably in competition with other buyers. Before contacting the bank, you may have negotiated a selling price that is lower than the original asking price. Occasionally, though, a bank's decision can be delayed by an ungainly procedure called the appraisal process.

■ *KEY POINT: The first criterion of the bank is the value of the property.*
■ *CAUTION NOTE: The appraisal process takes time.*

As required by the Federal Reserve Board, which oversees fair-credit standards, an independent appraiser approved by the bank must determine the value of the property. This is done at a cost to you as the borrower of between $200 and $400. As this amount adds significantly to your closing costs, you will want to minimize the possibility of errors. Appraisers, who may see dozens of properties each day, and perhaps a hundred or more weekly, are prone to mistakes. Sometimes, appraisers unfamiliar with a neighborhood make invalid comparisons with other recently sold properties. Note that you always have the right to have a copy of the appraisal. Ask for it in writing—a useful tool in dealing with the lender and seller.

Appraisals done by in-house staff—not common under new banking guidelines—are not as thoroughly researched or as detailed as those you would get from an independent appraiser. Bank appraisals are quick, one-page studies based primarily on the square footage of the building and its age. These "quicky" appraisals often do not consider such tangible values as the neighborhood in which the house is located or its style or antique value. Because of the brevity of such reports, recent banking guidelines require an independent appraisal.

■ *CAUTION NOTE: Staff appraisers are prone to mistakes.*

What you will learn here is how to short-circuit or "support" this appraisal process.

The second financial criterion critical in satisfying a bank is the availability of money to repay the mortgage loan. The statement of sources for funds will include you and your spouse's (or other cobuyer[s]) employment income and any other income you may have from investments or non-job-related sources that can help meet monthly loan payments. This disclosure considers where you stand in the overall financial picture, including your current assets and liabilities and income and expenses. This is the second requirement of the bank for which you can prepare.

■ *KEY POINT: Satisfy the bank with a detailed disclosure of your finances.*

The third and most important criterion loan officers use in considering a loan is whether it will be profitable for the bank. This requirement should be obvious, but many borrowers overlook it. All internal decisions by a bank on any mortgage application take profitability into account.

The interest rate on your mortgage varies with the cost of money in the overall marketplace. It affects the decisions by any particular bank on what interest rate and other costs you will be charged.

■ *KEY POINT:* *The loan must be profitable for the bank.*

There's a cost to money. A bank that doesn't get a return on what it charges you will have a difficult time paying back its depositors—or the larger money pools from which it borrows money.

Let's see what each of these three principles means in practice. An understanding of what you can do to satisfy your bank's criteria will give you a favorable decision in the quickest amount of time.

PREPARING THE SUREFIRE PROPOSAL

The following is one of the simplest and most practical ways to assure mortgage financing. Professionals have used it for years. Whether you are buying a small apartment building, major shopping center, or a family home, you use a short, three- to six-page proposal to request a loan. By following the three steps named earlier, you will almost always gain a quick, favorable decision.

■ *KEY POINT:* *A brief proposal assures favorable commitment quickly.*

This proposal addresses the bank's internal decisions in a neutral, nonthreatening way. It provides the loan officers with information that they would otherwise have to gain on their own in a time-consuming process of investigation. In the proposal that you will prepare, you must put down the information they need.

The bank may require you to rewrite the information on forms they provide, but if so, the presentation as well as the information will remain largely the same. This proposal also offers an intangible plus: Besides providing pertinent information so that the bank can honor your request, it demonstrates that you are a competent businessperson with whom the bank would wish to do business.

■ *KEY POINT: A bank is most likely to make a rapid, favorable decision with detailed property information.*

This intangible factor addresses an important side of the mortgage decision, the aspect that most bankers rarely talk about. The business of loaning money is not purely technical; it's partly emotional.

Don't think of the process as a matter of presenting a loan request to a computer. From the loan officer to the investment commitment to the appraiser, bankers are living, emotional people. Beyond the technical reasons to make or not make the loan, they base their decisions partly on emotional, intangible needs—the reasons undefinable.

■ *CAUTION NOTE: Banks often make emotional, nontechnical decisions.*

This proposal helps reduce any intangible need not to grant your loan by giving you added protection against extraneous or nontechnical reasons for rejection. You will know that if you do not get the loan, it will be because your $10,000 income without any savings doesn't support a $250,000 home loan, or because the $500,000 home you want is located in a neighborhood of dilapidated rowhouses.

■ *KEY POINT: A mortgage proposal assures reasonable success.*

Let's look closely at what each of the major parts of this proposal entails.

Jumping the Gun on the Appraisal

First, we address the problem of value or quality of a property. Don't pretend to be a professional appraiser, but you can, in a qualified way, follow some of the principles appraisers use. With minimal research, you often can do a more thorough job than the appraiser. You can certainly find the same information the appraiser would reference in making a formal report.

■ *KEY POINT:* *Provide the bank with a miniappraisal.*

The most important criterion in determining the value of a property is how the negotiated price compares with the selling prices of recently purchased properties similar in size, neighborhood, and amenities.

This comparison is not difficult for you to make. If you are going through a real estate broker in buying a property, he or she can help you with information on recent sales. If you don't have a broker, the job is still relatively easy. Most real estate offices keep specific information on sold properties and are often willing to share it with you. All you need to do is pick out from their "sold" file properties of similar size and compare the data against your property (e.g., number of bedrooms and baths, dining room, study, living room, kitchen, one- or two-car garage, and other specific amenities such as extra land area, swimming pool, gazebo). Look for sales within the past year, preferably the past six months, that will duplicate as closely as possible the house or income property you wish to purchase.

■ *KEY POINT:* *Comparable sales confirm value.*

Another criterion is the general economic level of the neighborhood in which your house is located. Figure 1.1 provides a sample to follow in obtaining two or three comparable prices of

COMPARABLE VALUE ANALYSIS

	Property 1		Property 2		Property 3	
Address	65 Armister		34 Weems		9 Bruiet	
Date of sale	January 1994		June 1994		May 1994	
Sale Price		$91,500		$89,500		$81,500
Adjustments	*(−)*	*(+)*	*(−)*	*(+)*	*(−)*	*(+)*
Adjustment for date	0	1,500	0	0	0	0
Age/condition	0	0	0	0	0	3,500
Size/utility	6,000	0	0	0	3,000	0
Kitchen/bath	1,200	0	0	0	1,200	0
Porch/garage	0	0	0	1,500	0	2,000
Site/location	2,500	0	2,500	0	0	0
Other/amenity	0	1,200	0	1,200	0	1,200
Subtotals	*$8,200*	*$94,200*	*$2,500*	*$94,200*	*$4,200*	*$88,200*
Adjustment Totals		*$86,000*		*$89,700*		*$84,000*

Comparable value shown by market = $86,500

Note: Properties similar to property being financed are listed and adjusted to match subject property as closely as possible. Adjusted values are then averaged to show rough value. In this way, what you pay for a property is supported by common-sense facts such as selling prices, size, and location adjustments in the marketplace. No matter how large the property, this appraisal technique can be used to justify value.

Figure 1.1.   Sample chart showing comparable properties.

properties. The analysis shows comparable features, selling price, and date of sale.

Photographs of the properties will help but are not essential. A professional appraiser adds and subtracts specific dollar amounts to make the comparable houses exactly equal to the subject house. You may not be able to match prices exactly; you are simply giving the bank information on several sold properties that are comparable in physical characteristics to the property you wish to buy. This comparison, more than anything can justify the price that you have agreed to pay for your property.

It is invaluable information in guiding your bank to affirm the value of the property you wish to buy. Too often, conservative bankers will turn down a loan just because they don't have this information to go on.

■ *CAUTION NOTE: Use selling prices only.*

In picking out properties that match yours, don't choose similar sale prices. Look for properties that are comparable in nature (physical condition, neighborhood, and sale in a similar economic climate). Then, and only then, those selling prices should be able to put your property in a favorable light.

If these properties have all sold in the past six months, the current market should be similar to that under which they sold.

This miniappraisal, based on information you can easily obtain from local real estate people, will go a long way in encouraging a favorable decision by the bank. The value of the property is often the key factor in the mortgage lender's decision.

■ *KEY POINT: Property value is the most important criterion in granting a loan.*

This miniappraisal is significant. When you get a copy of the independent appraiser's formal appraisal, you can pick up on inconsistencies. You can spot if the appraiser used as a comparable property a similar-size house and lot three miles away but far less in value because of being in a different school district. You may then request a second opinion that can cause the bank to override the appraiser's estimate of value.

Further, your knowledge of the appraisal process will help if the formal appraisal happens to come in low and you need a talk with the seller; someone anxious to close a deal may be happy to drop the price if the property is appraised for less.

Your Own Financial Profile

The second part of the proposal is an outline of your assets and your income. It's nothing more than an organized financial profile of yourself that goes a long way toward speeding up the mortgage process.

This financial part of the proposal is easy to prepare. The sample shown in Figure 1.2 is basic but includes all major groups that you will need. On the first half of the page will be your balance sheet, specifically listing your assets and liabilities, plus net worth, which should equal each other. On the second half will be your income and expense statement detailing annual earnings and costs (see Figure 1.2).

■ *KEY POINT: An asset and liability statement outlines your financial status.*

In addition, many lenders require "W-2" forms or federal and state tax filings for the previous two years. These should accompany your proposal. Further information often requested may include a recent paycheck stub, copies of bank account statements for the past two months, verification and explanation of the sources for the down payment, and a copy of the sales contract signed by both parties.

■ *CAUTION NOTE: Don't omit any pertinent financial data.*

Let's understand something about your financial situation. You don't have to be worth a fortune to get a mortgage loan. You don't even need a long history of annual income, nor do you need to make a huge salary. You need to make enough money to afford payments if the property is to be your home; perhaps less, if rental income will more than cover these payments.

■ *KEY POINT: Wealth and large income are important but not critical.*

Some lenders look approvingly at upward of 50%—although 30% to 40% is more common—of your total income going toward mortgage payments. Even if you buy an apartment building or a commercial block for hundreds of thousands of dollars, your income is often of secondary importance when purchasing the property. The actual income from the apartments or commercial tenants is what will pay the loan.

```
                 PERSONAL FINANCIAL PROFILE
Income Statement:
─────────────────────────────────────────────────────────────
Employment earnings (husband and wife)              $27,000
Extra services income                                 4,500
Interest income                                       1,100
Net rental income                                     3,100
Other income                                              0
   Total annual income                              $35,700
                                                    ═══════
Expense Statement:
─────────────────────────────────────────────────────────────
Rent                                                $10,800
Utilities                                             3,800
Telephone                                               700
Babysitter                                              800
Food                                                  4,500
Car                                                   2,400
Educational expenses                                  1,250
Insurance                                             2,000
Loans                                                 4,000
Travel                                                2,500
Miscellaneous                                         1,000
   Total annual expenses                            $33,750
                                                    ═══════

                       BALANCE SHEET
Assets:
─────────────────────────────────────────────────────────────
Cash in checking accounts                           $ 1,100
Cash in savings account                               2,300
Money due                                               800
Loans owed by others                                  1,500
Stock owned                                           4,500
Value of life insurance                                 300
Real estate owned                                         0
Cars                                                  6,500
Personal property                                     3,500
Other assets                                          1,300
   Total assets                                     $21,800
                                                    ═══════
Liabilities:
─────────────────────────────────────────────────────────────
Accounts payable                                    $ 1,100
Notes payable                                         9,500
Income taxes                                          1,300
Mortgages                                                 0
Other debts                                             800
   Total liabilities                                $12,700
      Net worth (assets minus liabilities)          $ 9,100
                                                    ═══════
```

Figure 1.2. Sample financial profile—liabilities and income and expenses and personal assets.

■ *KEY POINT: Rental income of an investment property pays the mortgage.*

If you're married, make sure you list both your own and your spouse's earnings. Lenders accept the total annual income of both spouses. Just detail this information separately to show the source of each.

Your wages may come from a variety of sources. Some of it may come from a direct hourly or annual wage. Some may come from extra self-employment such as consulting or making furniture. The point is to list every source of income. List interest from savings accounts and capital amounts under your assets. Insert both in the income section. Unemployed persons have received mortgages based solely on trust fund income.

■ *KEY POINT: Your income can come from different sources.*

All a bank wants is to be assured that your monthly loan payments will be met. It comes back to one of the truths about small bankers. They don't want to foreclose. If they are adequately satisfied you can meet the mortgage payments, even if it is a big sock out of your income, they are likely to grant you the loan.

People often worry about their credit. This worry is largely overdone. Even if you've had credit problems in the past, your present economic situation is more important. The loan is made today under current economic conditions. Most mortgage lenders are called "equity lenders," that is, they're concerned that the security of their loan be in the value of the property. Your ability to make the loan payments is still required but is secondary to the bank's overall exposure of funds in the real estate itself. That's why finding out the value of the property is more critical than showing extensive reserves on your financial statement.

■ *KEY POINT: Credit is not as important as the value of the property.*

If you have had credit problems in the past, mention this fact in your proposal. The lender will be more receptive to an accommodation if you are forthright. However, you must address any negative information on your financial statement. The most painless way is to include the information as part of your proposal. Don't wait for the loan officer to ask you. Giving this information up front, even if it's not all good, will go a long way toward gaining credibility with the bank.

■ *CAUTION NOTE: Mentioning any credit plight helps defuse its effect on the lender.*

■ *KEY POINT: Divulging personal financial information gives you credibility with a bank.*

If you have many assets and make ample income in relation to the mortgage you're requesting, that's fine. If not, remember that your financial condition is not the most important criterion on which the bank bases a mortgage decision. You go a long way by addressing your status truthfully in the proposal.

In fact, banks have less loan trouble with customers who have small amounts of income from a variety of sources than from those with income from a single source that might be gone if the person loses his or her job. Several-source incomes show the customer is willing to work at a variety of tasks to pay debts.

■ *KEY POINT: Banks like multiple sources of income.*

So don't try to outguess the bank. Put down your assets and your income truthfully. As long as you, or the property, can amply meet payments, you will likely get the loan.

■ *KEY POINT: Banks look for ability to meet payments.*

Making Sure the Lender Gets a Fair Share

At this point in your proposal, you have addressed two major criteria that lenders look at closely: the property and the borrower. The last consideration, the lender's profit, may appear to be out of control, and to some degree it is.

What you must keep in mind is that once you pass the first two criteria you still may not get a mortgage unless the bank is going to make money from the loan.

■ *CAUTION NOTE: Banks must assure their profit.*

Their profit may appear automatic. After all, they charge you a lot of interest, don't they? Yes, but they must compete with other banks to give you the superior deal. The answer to this dilemma comes in negotiating specific loan and mortgage terms.

The type of loan you request (conventional loan, adjustable-rate mortgage, variable-payment loan, or some other mortgage instrument)—combined with the particular interest rate and length of time under which the loan will be paid back—will be the factors that determine whether the bank can make a fair profit as well as give you a fair deal.

■ *KEY POINT: Banks profit from a variety of factors: interest rate, length of loan, service fees, and prepayment stipulations.*

This does not mean that you should (or can) offer the bank more interest than it would expect. Banks state interest rates for various types of loans. These rates may change weekly, either falling or rising depending on the economic climate.

To achieve a mutually helpful loan, you can negotiate many kinds of mortgage instruments and terms with each bank. Much information on this subject follows in the rest of this book. Being armed with knowledge of what mortgages are all about is the prime way for you to assure that you can construct a fair deal—a profitable covenant for the bank as well as one that is helpful for you.

■ *CAUTION NOTE: Central to negotiation is knowing the types of mortgages available.*

The succeeding chapters describe many ways to construct a loan. No longer are mortgages just the traditional kind, where interest rate and term were fixed and nonnegotiable. Adjustable-rate mortgages, variable-payment mortgages, blanket mortgages, trust deeds, and variations of these instruments are among the many kinds of loans you can negotiate with mortgage lenders.

■ *KEY POINT: A variety of loans are available.*

Not every lender subscribes to every kind of mortgage. Your task is to find out the different options within a particular bank and make a particular request within that framework. Figure 1.3 shows a sample loan request.

This request should assure fairness for both you and the bank. Your concern for the bank's reasonable profitability is one of the best ways for you to gain control.

■ *KEY POINT: Concern for the bank's profitability helps gain a favorable loan commitment.*

Selling Yourself to Your Banker

The final step in your proposal is to write a short cover letter. This need be nothing more than a brief description of how much money you will need and what you intend to buy. You

---

LOAN REQUEST

I request an 80% mortgage loan of $93,000 at an interest rate of 9% for a term of 20 years. I understand from preliminary discussions during our prequalifying stage with you that if I pay two percentage points at the closing you will reduce your customary rate of 9.75% to 9%. I also request that your prepayment penalty of 3% of the loan balance paid to the bank at the time of sale be reduced to 1.5% after three years and no penalty charged after ownership of five years.

Figure 1.3.   Sample loan request.

could also mention any extenuating circumstances, such as work to be done with the property and how much it might cost. Like the other parts of our proposal, this cover letter should be easy for the bank's loan officers to read and understand. The format, while simple, helps show you are a responsible person with whom the bank can confidently do business.

■ *KEY POINT: The cover letter capsulizes three points: value, finances, and profitability.*

The letter can also refer to the three major parts of the proposal. Use short, simple terms and state your request clearly and concisely. The cover letter should never be more than one page. It is not the place for you to ramble on with extraneous details about why you desperately need this money. Business writing should be succinct and appealing. This letter is not the place for extensive prose, long words, or detailed descriptions. Remember, the proposal condenses a major financial undertaking into a simple, easy-to-understand request. Figure 1.4 shows a sample cover letter.

■ *KEY POINT: Write a brief statement in clear English.*

With such information, your banker does not need to take a long time to decide. Often, favorable decisions are granted almost immediately. Doubtful decisions take more time. The purpose of the proposal is to tip the balance in your favor. It is a logical presentation of factual information—a superb way to sell yourself to your banker.

■ *KEY POINT: A well-constructed proposal is likely to tip the mortgage decision in your favor.*

Convincing the Homeowner

This book is not only about getting loans from institutional lenders. It also explains now to negotiate a loan with the person from whom you are purchasing the property. You will use

Mr. Michael Sigafoos, Junior Officer
American National Savings
Westchester, Columbus, Naples, Berkeley

Dear Mr. Sigafoos,

   Thank you for the time you have shared with me explaining your loan policies and the different types of mortgages available. At this time, I would like to follow up on our talks with a formal proposal for a mortgage.
   I have placed a deposit on a single-family residence in Heritage Estates in neighboring Winston. The owner and I have agreed to a selling price of $110,000. I intend to put down in cash 20% of the purchase price. I am borrowing $7,000 from my family to add to $15,000 of my own funds. Therefore, I would like to borrow $88,000 for a 20-year term.
   Enclosed I include recent selling prices for properties similar to the one I'm buying. Since I'm buying several months after these other properties have closed, I believe I'm getting excellent value and will provide the bank with ample security.
   I am also enclosing a detailed record of my income and expenses and a full disclosure of my assets and liabilities. I believe I can easily meet the needs of monthly payments on this mortgage.
   I do hope you will act favorably on this request.

                                                    Sincerely,

Figure 1.4.   Cover letter.

a different proposal since you do not need to convince the seller of the value of his or her property in comparison with other recent sales. However, it's helpful to you to give him or her an understanding of your financial position. In this way, you show the seller your ability to meet payments.

■ *KEY POINT: The proposal to the seller need not contain appraisal information.*

You can also outline the different terms with which the loan might be constructed, showing how they might benefit the seller and produce a profit.

Your request for the seller to take back a mortgage has two parts. The first part shows your financial stability, and the second the benefits he or she will derive from holding this loan.

The sample letter shown in Figure 1.5 indicates how to entice a seller. In this situation, you can be less impartial than you needed to be with your banker. You don't need as much detail on your assets and liabilities and income and expenses. You need to show in a general way only what the seller might want to know, perhaps offering more information if your proposal is accepted.

■ *KEY POINT: The letter to the seller is more flexible.*

In this letter you might mention what kind of mortgage you would negotiate, the interest rate, and such terms that might be of advantage to both parties. In particular, stress those that might appeal to the seller. Perhaps you could pay off a large portion of the loan at a date sooner than the full term of the loan. Perhaps you could bring out details of the amount of interest paid over the term of the mortgage. The interest is usually a considerable amount and enticing to a seller. This letter can be more obvious in its sales effort to get the seller to agree to give you the mortgage.

■ *KEY POINT: The letter to the owner can sell more.*

Other information in this book, particularly in Chapter 9, will give you many ideas for structuring mortgages with sellers.

A proposal is almost a requirement in buying a commercial or investment property. The seller of an income property is a businessperson who is more familiar with financial proposals and more experienced at constructing and arranging a mortgage for you.

LETTER TO SELLER

Mr. Jack Thompson

Dear Mr. Thompson,

Thank you for showing me your property last week. It's a fine house and shows the care you and Mrs. Thompson have given it over the years.

I would like to do what I can to purchase your home. You're asking $79,000, which is reasonable if I can be helped. Bank financing is very scarce with high interest rates this year. For me to purchase, I would like to ask you if I could take over your existing loan, which as you told me has a balance of $34,000 at an interest rate of 8½% with 12 years left to pay. Further, if you could lend me a second mortgage of $29,000, I could pay you 11% interest. I have myself and what I can get from other sources just under $16,000, a substantial amount of equity, to put down.

I know you didn't expect to give someone a second mortgage, but I hope to make it attractive to you. The interest rate of 11% is better than most money-market opportunities and guarantees you income each month. This second is backed by the security of your property. Also if you will agree to a payment period of 20 years so my monthly payments will not be too high, I will agree to pay this loan balance off in 6 years or sooner if I can refinance the balance of both loans at 10% or less.

I include a financial statement showing my income and expenses and assets and liabilities to show you I can meet payments on both loans.

I know you're anxious to move to your daughter's home in Minnesota. If my proposal is agreeable, you can start packing. I'll be ready to close within the week.

Sincerely,

Figure 1.5. Letter to seller.

■ *KEY POINT: The seller of investment property needs a proposal detailing your financial information.*

Often you can get a definite commitment from an individual seller on a mortgage request immediately. The written proposal outlining your formal request is designed to assure the minimal amount of time necessary for a seller to make up his or her mind. As with a bank, it is your opportunity to get a favorable decision in the fastest time.

■ *KEY POINT: A proposal accompanying a purchase offer often guarantees a quick decision by the seller.*

How to Finance a Property in Any Market

Writing a mortgage proposal is valuable in any economic climate. When mortgage money is plentiful, it will help you negotiate the prize interest rate. When money is tight, it will help you get a superior deal with the seller.

Either way, in good times or bad, your assurance in securing a favorable decision on a mortgage request, whether it involves a bank or seller, is to outline specific written terms addressing major points to satisfy the lender. Security of the property, ability to repay the loan, and acknowledgment that the loan will be profitable are the three points essential in negotiating a loan under any market conditions. Often, by addressing them, you can get a superb deal on a mortgage, while someone else in similar circumstances does not.

■ *KEY POINT: A mortgage proposal helps you negotiate a loan when funds are scarce.*

In the next chapter, we will discuss the benefit of being prepared by prequalifying for the mortgage.

PREQUALIFYING FOR A MORTGAGE 2

By prequalifying for a mortgage, you can save time as well as avoid rejection. Many lenders give buyers a letter certifying their ability to qualify for a specific level of loan.

This prequalification statement indicates how much you can afford. You won't waste time looking at property outside your price range.

■ *KEY POINT:* *Prequalification speeds the application process.*

Additionally, this prequalification gives nervous sellers assurance you can secure the loan. It not only shows your creditworthiness but proves you have opened negotiations with a specific lender. Further, the limits it sets may provide a distinct advantage when seeking acceptance of an offer less than full price.

■ *KEY POINT:* *Prequalification supports your creditworthiness in negotiating with sellers.*

Prequalification can also firm up the recommended amount for the down payment. If you desire to reduce the down payment in the range of 5% to 10% instead of the normal 15% to 20%, prequalification helps show you can gain the mortgage insurance often required for the lower down payment.

■ *KEY POINT:* *Prequalification helps in negotiating lower down payments.*

HOW YOU CAN PREQUALIFY

As part of the prequalifying process, a lender will ask you for financial information—from your income and cost of living to what present assets you now own and what liabilities are against them. He or she will discuss various mortgage plans you can afford.

Based on your financial status, the lender will give you in writing or, as often, a verbal understanding of the maximum you should pay for a house as well as what particular loan plan you would fit into.

■ *KEY POINT: Prequalification sets loan parameters.*

A formal prequalification does not lock you into a particular program but gives you an idea of a range to target in house-hunting, both in money as well as choice of loan.

REAL ESTATE BROKERS CAN HELP

If you happen to be seeking a house through a broker, he or she can often help track down additional strategies, such as seller financing and alternatives offered at different lenders. A mortgage lender can only prequalify you in connection with that institution's own offerings. Characteristics that may qualify you at one bank may not be acceptable in another. Or, a bank may slot you into an adjustable-rate mortgage, whereas you might be better off with a fixed-rate loan.

Sometimes contacting a real estate sales agent is the best approach for this service because then you can survey the broadest range of alternative strategies. The agent may also know the superior alternatives in government programs such as the Federal Housing Administration (FHA), Farmers Home Administration (FmHA), Veterans Administration (VA), or other special assistance programs.

■ *KEY POINT:* *Use real estate sales agents to point you to worthy mortgage plans.*

PREQUALIFICATION PROFILE

The prequalification profile is similar to the loan proposal discussed in Chapter 1. The major difference, however, is that the property is not yet secured and only general information is available on what loan might be most helpful for you in a particular property.

The prequalification profile does address two major points: (1) financial information about you, and (2) a general targeting of the lender and type of loan that will best fit your needs.

■ *KEY POINT:* *Prequalifying means gathering your financial information and targeting lender and type of loan.*

The following sections provide a breakdown of five critical points you must address in the prequalification process: (1) available cash, (2) income, (3) equity, (4) credit, and (5) character.

Available Cash

A big question is, do you have the cash for the down payment? In the past, you could borrow this money quietly from your family and no one would know the difference, or care. Now with full financial disclosure and probing credit evaluations, just where down payment funds come from has become important to the lender. Specifically, the lender wants to be sure that you can form capital within your own devices as well as not be bound to anyone else for additional repayment.

If you do not have a full down payment, this does not mean that you will be unable to get mortgage approval. Parents, other family members, and inheritance are sources that often win approval from the lender. When part or all of your down payment comes from a personal loan or gift from your family, banks can be edgy. Lenders traditionally require you to have earned your down payment, although many have eased these restrictions. When you do have to get help with the down payment, loan officers may look more closely at your credit history as well as your sources of income. What is most important is that enough equity will be put down on the property to assure the lender's risk.

Income

Whether you have enough income to make the monthly mortgage payment is critical. As explained in Chapter 1, income can come from a variety of sources. Lenders understand borrowers work part-time jobs, have investment income, or may be self-employed. However, after deducting basic or required expenses, they want to make sure you have enough money to satisfy the mortgage payments. To do this, they may employ an affordability ratio. This ratio relates to housing expense and is easy to compute:

$$\text{Affordability ratio} = \frac{\text{Monthly housing payment}}{\text{Monthly income}}$$

The monthly housing payment includes not only the mortgage payment itself but property taxes and insurance plus any housing-related costs such as mortgage insurance. Monthly income includes legitimate income from all sources.

The housing expense ratio may vary between 25% and 35%. Strong income and credit and a large down payment may qualify you for a higher ratio, whereas a weakness in any area would require the lender to desire a lower ratio.

For example, assume you borrow $80,000 at 7.5% for 20 years. The monthly payment (principal and interest) for this amount is $462 per month. Property taxes, property insurance, and mortgage insurance equal a monthly cost of $275, making your monthly housing expense total $737. Divide your monthly housing payment by your monthly income of $2,543 and you get an affordability ratio of 29%.

$$\text{Affordability ratio} = \frac{\$737}{\$2,543} = 0.29 \text{ or } 29\%$$

The application of this ratio may vary depending on the requirements of each lender. But its basic premise is that a reasonable percentage of your income should be available to satisfy the mortgage and housing costs.

An additional ratio often used by mortgage lenders is called the debt ratio. Here you add any additional installment debt to the monthly housing payment and divide by monthly income to establish a total debt ratio. This ratio, which will range slightly higher than the affordability ratio, is often used to determine upper limits because conventional loans that may be sold to Freddie Mac (Federal Home Loan Mortgage Corporation; FHLMC) or Fannie Mae (Federal National Mortgage Association; FNMA) must be under .35 to .38.

$$\text{Debt ratio} = \frac{\text{Housing payment} + \text{installment debt}}{\text{Monthly income}}$$

Principal and interest	$
Property taxes, insurance	
Personal loans	
Car payments	
Credit cards	
Education loans	
Total monthly debt payments	$

$$\text{Debt ratio} = \frac{\$}{\$} = .\quad \text{or}\quad \%$$

Using these ratios helps you focus on why it's important to lay out your finances in the prequalification stage—assessing income from all sources and totaling all proposed expenses.

Equity

As we saw in constructing the mortgage proposal (see Chapter 1), equity is the asset part of "assets and liabilities." In addition to the cash you have for a down payment and closing costs, it is the other reserves of cash in savings accounts, CDs, stocks, bonds, and life insurance cash values. It also includes equity you have in other property, your car, or even a boat or specialized piece of equipment.

Again, as with other criteria, a lender may look favorably on strength in one area to balance for weakness in another. Free and clear ownership of income property or another house or land may compensate for a modest income.

Credit

Next to down payment and income, good credit comes close in importance to qualifying for a loan. Paying bills on time—present mortgage or rent, car payments, credit cards—goes a long way to ease a lender's fear about their being paid back regularly. However, if you have had a setback in the past 2 years, you can lessen its negative effect by telling the lender the circumstances of your delay and explaining why it's unlikely to happen again.

Your credit is usually checked by an outside service. A typical report by companies such as TRW provides a personal credit profile on you. It will include a full analysis of your credit history including pertinent technical information such as current and previous addresses, Social Security number, employment record, record of mortgage or installment payments, legal judgments against you, as well as any recent inquiries about your credit.

Credit reports may sound spooky, and perhaps they should be for someone trying to hide something. For most of us, they are fairly benign and a necessary part of the loan process. Any discrepancies or missteps in financial matters that do show up on the credit report can usually be repaired by explaining what occurred and how you have corrected the problem.

Credit reporting is governed by the Fair Credit Reporting Act, originally enacted in 1971. Its purpose is to guarantee that consumers are treated fairly and that information sent out about their credit standing is accurate. The law outlines procedures to be followed in cases of dispute, as well as who may legitimately receive information and under what circumstances. If you wish to get a copy of your credit profile, you may do so by so requesting it, in writing, from the particular service. Should you find inaccuracies, the credit service is bound to investigate the discrepancy factually.

Character

No matter how well the numbers stack up and appear to give you a clean financial bill of health, a weighty criterion in gaining a lender's approval is that elusive quality known as character.

Banking is not number crunching as many assume. Contrary to popular opinion, it is not a computer formula that decides who gets a loan. The final decision maker is always a person. The banker as lender likes to feel secure that he or she is lending the bank's money to someone with personal strength and integrity—a person who, regardless of misfortune, will continue to satisfy the mortgage debt. Too often, mortgages have gone to people with sufficient capital and income who still default on their debt.

Lenders must judge whether the borrower has the resolve to pay his or her bills. Someone who proves that he or she is forthright and conscientious can make up for being short on credit or cash.

Display the worthiness of your own character by doing what you say you will do. Show an attentive and respectful nature in your meetings with the lender, be prompt with all appointments, and provide all requested information. Show commitment to your goal of gaining a mortgage. Your personal enthusiasm can go a long way.

As with the mortgage proposal, the prequalification profile should be in writing. From the loan officer's point of view, the more data you can put in writing to support the loan request, the more likely it is to be approved.

■ *KEY POINT: Detail all financial information and sources in writing.*

Your prequalification profile doesn't need to be as elaborate as a mortgage proposal although much of the information will eventually be part of the formal proposal, once you find the specific property you wish to buy. You can't, in fact, provide your own credit report. However, you can put down on paper a statement of your assets and liabilities as well as your annual income and expenses. You can detail many of these sources and provide names, addresses, and telephone numbers for employment and income.

HOW YOU CAN (ALMOST) ALWAYS GET YOUR MORTGAGE

The best way to assure you will get your mortgage is to be forthright and persistent. Forthrightness means that you will be open with the financial information the seller or mortgage lender needs to consider before giving you a mortgage commitment. Absolute honesty is essential in your financial disclosure statement as well as any appraisal information you present that backs up the value of the property. If a banker thinks that you have inflated figures or made other exaggerations, he or she is likely to use extensive information at his or her disposal to discredit your presentation and reject your request. It is almost better to understate possessions so in the mind of the lender you have even more credibility than initially apparent.

■ *KEY POINT: Forthrightness and honesty gain credibility with the bank.*

The other way to secure a mortgage is persistence. You must show the lender, whether an institution or seller, that you are anxious for his or her favorable approval. You don't need to engulf, but you should let the lender know that you are always available to provide more information. State your willingness to be interviewed and to provide help in verifying the information you have given.

■ *KEY POINT: Persistence keeps bankers conscious of your interest.*

When you begin your initial meeting with the banker, ask what loans and interest rates are available. You may or may not have found the right property, but even before you find what you want, it's good to start shopping for the bank that offers the preferable terms and interest rates.

■ *KEY POINT: Preliminary shopping for your loan will yield information and personal contacts.*

If, before you buy, you know what bank you wish to do business with, so much the better. Comparison shopping on types of loans and their terms and conditions will help you decide. Often you need to be persistent in getting the one with which you can make the best deal. Make contact, then, with as many loan officers in your area as you can. This book describes many kinds of mortgages and their conditions to help you negotiate with a bank or seller.

THE SECRET OF GETTING A QUICK MORTGAGE

Prequalification will assure you a mortgage commitment from a bank before you decide on a property. If you decide on a bank before you conclude preliminary negotiations (type of loan, interest rates, financial situation), you won't have to start from scratch in negotiating with a lender when you are ready to apply for a particular mortgage. You've already done the most of the work needed. That's what's so valuable about prequalifying.

■ *KEY POINT: Shop for the loan before you contract to buy property.*

At this point, you've laid the groundwork for getting a favorable decision. Once you choose the property, all you need to do is to assure the lender that the purchase price of the property is reasonable and that the loan doesn't conflict with the bank's lending guidelines.

This may look simple, but it is the most effective way to achieve a quick mortgage commitment. It's the method used by professional investors who wouldn't think of negotiating for a property without first having talked with a mortgage lender about the parameters within which mortgages are given and the interest rates and terms available.

■ *KEY POINT: Professionals always shop banks and types of mortgages first.*

More and more individual, nonprofessional bank customers are taking this approach. Whether you are buying a single-family house, vacation home, or investment property for the first time, initially set up a working relationship with a mortgage lender. Then, follow up with a formal proposal when you find the right property.

■ *KEY POINT: Set up contact by prequalifying with the banker before submitting a formal proposal on a specific property.*

When you go back to the lender with your mortgage proposal, you are not a stranger. He or she knows your financial condition, even the approximate amount you can be lent. You, in turn, know in a general way what terms are available—the types of loan and interest rates. You can be certain that a quicker decision will be forthcoming than if you walked into the bank and started communication cold.

Being prepared can also help you lock in an interest rate. Lenders have been known to delay completing paperwork because rates are about to be raised. By delaying, they are able to impose a higher rate. However, if you provide an adequate proposal, you protect yourself against such delaying tactics. You have done the lender's work for him or her by coming to the table fully prepared. Nothing could be a better negotiating point for locking in the lowest possible interest rate.

■ *KEY POINT: Preliminary contact with the banker helps assure quick approval.*

In this chapter, you have learned many secrets for getting an immediate, favorable mortgage. These principles—borrowed from the pros—are good practices to follow in shopping for a mortgage. You must be persistent in finding the superior bank with which to do business and in undertaking preliminary negotiations to satisfy the lender's concerns about the value of the property, your ability to repay the loan, and its mutual profitability. This approach will help ensure a favorable and quick mortgage commitment.

In Chapter 3, we will talk about the predominant types of mortgage and how each kind works. This information will enable you to pick the best loan for your needs.

ALL YOU NEED TO 3
KNOW ABOUT
MORTGAGES

To negotiate a speedy mortgage commitment, you need some basic knowledge about available mortgages that might work for you.

This chapter describes the major types of mortgage.

THE BASICS OF MORTGAGE FINANCING

A mortgage is a loan secured by property—a means of borrowing money. The mortgage agreement, held by a bank or seller, is a promise to a lender—bank or seller—that you will repay the loan including the accrued interest. The property you purchase is the major part of the security for the repayment of this loan.

■ *KEY POINT: A mortgage is a loan on a property.*

■ *KEY POINT: A mortgage agreement is the promise to repay.*

The buyer of the property is the borrower, called the mortgagor, who gives the mortgage as pledge for repayment. The lender receiving this pledge is the mortgagee, who holds the mortgage and receives payment on it from the mortgagor pledging the property.

■ *KEY POINT: The borrower gives the mortgage as pledge for repayment.*

The lender records the mortgage with the Registry of Deeds, or other governmental depository, as a legal document. This notice states that if the terms of the mortgage are not met, such as failure to repay on schedule or sale of the property, the holder of the mortgage (the lender) has a legal way, usually called foreclosure, to take possession of the property to satisfy the indebtedness.

■ *KEY POINT: Mortgages are recorded in legal depositories.*

■ *CAUTION NOTE: Upon default, foreclosure is a legal way for the lender to claim property.*

The loan lasts until the principal amount of the money plus interest is paid off. Then the mortgage is dissolved and the property is owned free and clear by the borrower.

■ *KEY POINT: The loan is dissolved when it is paid in full.*

THE BIG FOUR: THE BASIC TYPES OF MORTGAGES

How Conventional Mortgages Work

Most mortgages are called conventional mortgage loans. These include standard fixed- and variable-rate loans, both of which can be negotiated with a lending institution or the seller from whom you are buying the property.

The conventional mortgage doesn't carry any government guarantee. The loan is created by direct negotiation between you and a private bank or seller.

■ *KEY POINT: Conventional bank mortgages are private contracts.*

Most conventional mortgages have fixed interest rates that are constant throughout the term of the mortgage. The monthly payment doesn't vary for the life of the loan. Knowing that payments will never rise, that is, not being dependent on general economic conditions, gives you a measure of security.

■ **KEY POINT:** *Fixed interest and equal payments add up to security.*

A conventional mortgage has a fixed rate of interest. This means that if your first monthly payment is $535, it will be the same 20 years from now. This offers financial consistency. Each year, inflation eats away at the value of the dollar. It's easier in each succeeding year to get the money to make this fixed payment. A difficult amount in the first few years will be easier to pay as time goes on.

■ **KEY POINT:** *Fixed payments offer financial consistency.*

The disadvantage is that the mortgage is based on fixed interest rates. If interest rates go up over the term of the mortgage you benefit; if they go down, you lose.

■ **CAUTION NOTE:** *Fixed rates are bad for borrowers when rates go down.*

Sometimes you can renegotiate a conventional fixed-rate mortgage should interest rates go lower than your present rate. To make it worthwhile, there must be a strong difference that offsets special charges such as "points."

■ **KEY POINT:** *Conventional loans can be renegotiated.*

Another aspect of the conventional fixed-rate mortgage is that the amount of interest paid during the early years of the mortgage exceeds the amount of principal in each monthly payment. In the beginning, this interest consumes almost the entire payment, but in later years, this ratio shifts and the principal part of the payment far exceeds interest.

■ **CAUTION NOTE:** *In the beginning years of a loan, interest payments exceed principal.*

Table 3.1 shows how a conventional mortgage works over a term of 25 years. You can use this table as a guide for comparison with other forms of mortgages. You'll notice the borrower needs to reach some years into the mortgage before starting to pay off much of the balance. Although it took the full 25 years to pay off the original amount borrowed, a large amount of interest was paid over the full term. It will be useful to compare these percentages with other mortgage plans.

How ARMs Work

The high interest rates of the late 1970s and the early 1980s spurred the creation of diverse kinds of mortgages. Not only was money to lend out rather scarce but demand went down in proportion to the higher rate. To soften the blow of the higher rates, banks invented some ingenious devices and, in so doing, sought to protect themselves.

The most popular device, at least among the bankers, was the adjustable-rate mortgage, or ARM. Many new borrowers found themselves faced with this new mortgage. They had little choice;

Payment of principal and interest in a fixed-rate, conventional loan: $75,000 mortgage for 25 years at 8.5% interest.

Year	Annual Payment	Interest	Principal	Balance
1	$4,712	$2,910	$1,802	$73,198
2	4,712	2,838	1,874	71,323
3	4,712	2,763	1,949	69,374
4	4,712	2,685	2,027	67,347
5	4,712	2,604	2,108	65,239
6	4,712	2,520	2,192	63,047
10	4,712	2,148	2,564	53,368
15	4,712	1,594	3,119	38,927
20	4,712	919	3,793	21,363
25	4,712	99	4,614	0

Table 3.1. Conventional mortgage (hypothetical example).

banks made it easy to borrow this way and penalized those who still wanted a fixed rate.

■ *CAUTION NOTE: Banks invented adjustable mortgages to protect themselves.*

How does an ARM work? It's similar to the conventional mortgage except the rate of interest varies according to economic conditions. For example, if the interest rate you negotiate at the beginning of your mortgage is 8% and economic conditions, such as the supply of money, increased manufacturing ability, more trade with other countries, or simply lower taxes, cause that average cost of borrowing money to go down, the rate charged on a mortgage might drop to 6%.

The indicator chosen to monitor interest rates could be one of various governmental indexes, depending on the policy of your bank. For example, the 90-day Treasury bill (the interest rate the U.S. Treasury pays on short-term bonds) is a common index.

■ *KEY POINT: Adjustable-rate mortgages vary according to national indicators.*

It's hard to look at the adjustable-rate mortgage objectively and see it for what it is because the banks barrage us with favorable advertising. When ARMS started, rates were high, but in recent years, those rates have dropped off. What will happen when the rates rise again? There may be a lot of disappointed borrowers who will be hurt if they must start paying more each month.

The banks like ARMs when interest rates are high because they promote the loaning of money. Loans that otherwise couldn't be made because of the high interest rate can often be negotiated by convincing borrowers the rate will drop. And, as economic conditions improve, it often does so. Average interest rates of 16% to 18% have dropped into the range of 12% to 14%. What borrowers sometimes forget is that the opposite can happen too. When the general interest rate goes up, it can affect a mortgage by causing a dramatic jump in payments.

■ *CAUTION NOTE: Banks benefit with ARMs by passing on a rising interest rate.*

■ *KEY POINT: Borrowers benefit when rates fall.*

These are only words of caution, however. As with any mortgage, you get what you pay for. There are some decided advantages in opting for the ARM.

You must look into the exact terms and conditions of an ARM before reaching any final decision on whether it is best for you. Much can vary in an ARM, not only what national indicator the interest rate is tied to, but also the percentage that the mortgage can jump at any one time. For example, the indicators may jump 2% during a six-month period, but the conditions of your mortgage may allow the bank to increase your interest rate only 1%. This takes some of the sting out of the overall rise.

■ *CAUTION NOTE: Always study specific conditions that will make your rate rise or fall.*

In the same way that oil prices affect gasoline costs at the pump, banks tell you promptly about increases in the interest rate but are slower in negotiating your payment downward.

■ *CAUTION NOTE: Banks are quick to raise the rate but slow to lower it.*

You must be constantly vigilant. Sometimes, the slightly lower cost (for example, a percentage point or two) of an adjustable-rate mortgage is not always better than a conventional fixed rate. If your only benefit would be a rate two points lower than the fixed rate, you must compare what appears to be an advantage with the security of a fixed payment that will not vary regardless of the economic times. True, payments of the ARM may be more moderate in the beginning, but they may not remain easy to pay as time goes on. At least in theory, adjustable-rate payments of loans negotiated today could skyrocket in future years.

■ *KEY POINT: The initially lower interest in an ARM must be weighed against the long-term stability of a fixed-rate loan.*

■ *CAUTION NOTE: You need protection against the possibility of the ARM rate skyrocketing.*

However, in knowing their problems, you are armed in negotiating an ARM to your advantage. If an initially lower interest rate is important to you, and it should be, you can guard against harsh changes.

Protection against a large upward swing in the interest rate and payments is provided for in some ARM agreements. Some of these terms are either automatically within the mortgage agreement or can be negotiated into it by you. For example, the maximum amount that interest or payments can be increased each year should always be stated in an ARM agreement.

■ *KEY POINT: Negotiate the maximum upward swing.*

Table 3.2 will help you gauge the cost of an ARM. When comparing an ARM with a conventional mortgage, you might initially decide that if interest rates are likely to go up, you'd prefer

Beginning interest of 5½% on an adjustable-rate mortgage of $75,000 for 25 years.

Year	Rate (%)	Payment	Interest	Principal	Balance
1	5.5	$4,055	$1,879	$2,176	$72,824
2	6.0	4,161	1,991	2,170	70,720
3	6.0	4,161	1,930	2,230	68,490
4	6.5	4,268	2,030	2,238	66,436
5	7.0	4,377	2,121	2,256	64,414
10	8.0	4,599	2,006	2,593	52,908
15	9.0	4,827	1,709	3,118	39,447
20	10.0	5,062	1,140	3,922	22,562
25	11.0	5,302	143	5,159	0

Table 3.2.   Adjustable-rate mortgage (hypothetical example).

to get a fixed-rate loan and lock in the lower rate. However, if interest rates are expected to fall, you think an adjustable-rate mortgage would be preferable. There is some logic in this viewpoint, but beware of looking at the question this simply. Even the experts who suggest the probable direction of interest rates are often wrong. It is difficult to predict the future.

■ *CAUTION NOTE: It is almost futile to predict whether rates will rise or fall.*

Even the adage that interest rates rise when inflation is high and fall when inflation recedes is not always true. Too many other factors come into play, including world economic conditions or corporate failure, all of which may affect interest rates.

Despite the obvious advantages of an ARM, caution is suggested because its popularity may decrease as long-term interest rates become less stable and borrowers opt for the security of a fixed payment.

■ *CAUTION NOTE: ARMs may become less popular as interest rates become less stable.*

In negotiating any loan with a variable payment, make sure that upward swings are limited, not only in amount but in the length of time in which they can be enacted. And make sure there is a cap on the upward increase in mortgage interest. For example, you might have a $500-a-month payment at the beginning of the loan, and if necessary, you could handle a $700-a-month payment after two years. However, you may not want to be saddled with a $1,000 monthly payment if your original 8% rate skyrockets to 16%.

■ *KEY POINT: Negotiate a cap on how high the interest rate can rise.*

Approach ARMs with care. It may be cheaper to renegotiate a conventional fixed rate of interest downward than to struggle with the uncertainty of a rising mortgage rate. With a fixed-rate loan, you can assure stability, but you might, for example, have to start with an $800 payment.

Advertised by banks as a boon to consumers, ARMs more often benefit the lenders. You will learn more specifics about adjustable-rate loans in Chapter 8.

How Government Loans and Guarantees Work

The loans discussed in this book involve getting a mortgage from a bank or seller. However, when the government becomes involved in the loan process, a quick commitment is not always possible. It takes time for the government to move. You can speed up the process, but bringing in the government often means waiting one to three weeks to gain approval.

■ *CAUTION NOTE: Commitment is slow in government-approved loans.*

The Federal Housing Administration (FHA) and the Veterans Administration (VA) have loan programs that require only a minimum cash down payment or, in some cases, none. The VA (often referred to as "GI") loan is available for the purchase of homes. The VA loan specifies the amount of interest rate charged and the amount of money you can borrow. These loans do not usually require any down payment unless the price of the house exceeds a particular limit. The FHA loan limit is often somewhat less than that of the GI loan and requires a minimum down payment of 3% to 5%.

■ *KEY POINT: Government mortgages require only minimal down payments.*

Government loans afford a measure of security. The interest rate set by the government is frequently lower than the prevailing rates of the marketplace, and a government-approved loan appraiser must pass his or her often conservative judgment on your purchase.

■ *KEY POINT: The government has a rigid appraisal process.*

These loans can be difficult to negotiate. Banks simply don't like to make them because they can usually lend their money at a higher rate in a conventional mortgage. In practice, they have a guarantee from the government to be repaid should the borrower default, but as mentioned earlier in the book, foreclosures rarely take place except in dire circumstances.

■ *CAUTION NOTE: Banks shy away from government loans.*

When an institutional lender does make a loan of this type, it usually charges "points"—an extra two or three percentage points of the loan amount as a fee for making the loan. This increases the bank's yield and is only charged once to you. These factors must be taken into account when choosing the actual loan you may be eligible for.

■ *CAUTION NOTE: Extra percentage points based on the loan amount increase the bank's profit.*

How Seller Financing Works

One of the quickest ways to negotiate a mortgage commitment is to do business with the seller. Professional investors often do this with owners of commercial and residential buildings. In this era of high interest rates, it has also become popular with consumers buying smaller properties.

■ *KEY POINT: High rates have made seller financing popular.*

Often, the borrower approaches a bank on an as-need-to basis just in case financing negotiations with the seller should fail.

It's becoming more and more common for a seller of a home to participate in financing. If the seller has no current mortgage indebtedness on the property and owns it free and clear, you are in an excellent position to gain the seller's help.

■ *KEY POINT:* *"Free-and-clear" property eases seller financing.*

The seller could give you the entire first mortgage. For example, a retired couple moving to a resort area might like to hold a mortgage at current rates. Not only may they benefit tax-wise—not having to pay, through an installment sale (see Chapter 10), their income tax on the sale until the year in which they receive payment—but the money they will receive over the term of the mortgage is secured by the value of their former house, which they knew so well and loved.

■ *KEY POINT:* *When giving a mortgage, the seller can spread out taxes.*

Usually, the seller decides to help you financially when you negotiate the terms of the sale itself. You simply include in your purchase offer the condition that the seller take back all or a portion of the mortgage. The short-form purchase agreement, commonly used in the United States and shown in Figure 3.1, is the way to make this offer.

■ *KEY POINT:* *The deal on seller financing is negotiated at the same time as the sale.*

This seller becomes the lender. Loans with the seller are usually conventional with a fixed rate of interest. Rarely will the seller be sophisticated enough to deal with the complexities of giving you a swinging interest rate and variable payments. In any case, an adjustable loan may not be a good choice if you decide to finance with the seller.

■ *CAUTION NOTE:* *Seller financing is usually at a conventional fixed rate.*

The seller is not a professional lender. You may have versed yourself in the various types of mortgage and helpful conditions for financial institutions, but it's a one-time deal for the seller. To avoid confusion in the seller's mind, you must carefully

```
┌─────────────────────────────────────────────────────────────┐
│                                                               │
│               OFFER-TO-PURCHASE AGREEMENT                     │
│                                                               │
│                                    Date _____           │
│                                                               │
│                                                               │
│   I, _____, offer $_____ as a deposit on your prop-│
│   erty at _____ for the purchase price of $_____ to be re-│
│   turned to me if not accepted before _____. If accepted, in│
│   addition to this deposit I will put down the balance of _____% within│
│   10 days and will close on or before _____. Additional terms and con-│
│   ditions: Sale conditional upon buyer receiving financial approval from│
│   a local mortgage bank on or before _____. Seller will give buyer sec-│
│   ond mortgage for 8% of purchase price at 12% interest for 5 years.│
│                                                               │
│                                                               │
│                                                               │
│   _____     _____         │
│                                                               │
│   Buyer                       Seller                          │
│                                                               │
└─────────────────────────────────────────────────────────────┘
```

Figure 3.1. Short-form purchase agreement. (*Note:* Financing can be made part of a purchase offer.)

spell out the terms and benefits the seller will gain. Chapter 9 provides more information on seller financing.

■ *KEY POINT: Keep the financing proposal to the seller simple.*

When the seller takes the whole mortgage, you don't have to conjure up detailed information, such as comparable sales, on the value of the property. You may show the seller some assumptions of financial conditions. However, you avoid the paperwork required and often the more formal negotiations involved with an institutional lender. Getting the seller to take back the mortgage is the easiest and quickest way to secure a mortgage commitment.

■ *KEY POINT: You detail only your financial situation to the seller.*

Specific ways of arranging financing to benefit you and the seller are described in more detail in Chapter 9.

INNOVATIVE TECHNIQUES OF CREATIVE FINANCING

They say necessity is the mother of invention; it is no less true about financing. There are so many different ways to arrange the financing of real estate—houses, a second home, investment property, or land—that I would have to write an encyclopedia to tell about them all.

Many innovative techniques on creative financing are discussed in this book. They all have different names and angles that make them unique. Your key in benefiting from this information is to determine which plan will save you money.

For example, one of the more common techniques is to combine conventional financing with additional help from the seller. You may negotiate a fixed-rate or adjustable-rate mortgage with a bank for 80% of the purchase price and negotiate with the seller for another 10% to 15% as a second mortgage. This arrangement is desirable for the seller; it allows him or her to help the sale of the property and to gain some extra money in the form of interest over the term of the second mortgage. Second mortgages are usually for a far shorter term than an institutional loan and are perhaps a point more in interest than the average current mortgage interest rate.

■ *KEY POINT: Creative financing usually involves a combination of seller and bank financing.*

You, however, benefit by reducing your cash requirement for purchasing the house down to 5% to 10% of the selling price. In this way, you conserve your cash for needed improvements or as a reserve to help make future mortgage payments.

■ *KEY POINT: You can often commit less cash as a down payment through creative financing.*

The second mortgage by the seller is the simplest form of creative financing. It is also the most common and easiest to negotiate. Other techniques you've probably heard of, such as assuming the mortgage, purchase money mortgages, blanket mortgages, wraparounds, even the option with contract to buy, are only some of the innovative techniques described in this book—all of which can be negotiated in a short amount of time.

■ *KEY POINT: Second mortgages are a common way to finance creatively.*

What you need to do is choose from several alternatives and then tailor one or two of these to fit you and the seller. For example, you buy a 10-unit apartment building for $300,000 on which there already is a $180,000 first mortgage, a loan you cannot take over under the laws of your state. However, you can negotiate a wraparound mortgage with a minimal down payment of $10,000. The seller, in turn, gives you a mortgage of $290,000 on which you will make monthly payments to him. He, in turn, sends the portion of your monthly payment on the existing nonassumable loan of $180,000 to the bank that holds it.

■ *KEY POINT: A wraparound mortgage can often work when you can't assume an existing loan.*

This is similar to your taking over the responsibility of the existing mortgage and the seller giving you a second mortgage of $110,000. Often, it is not technically possible to assume a first mortgage; this is why another method has evolved to make the same transaction.

■ *CAUTION NOTE: Many existing mortgages are not assumable.*

The wraparound makes the deal. From the seller's point of view, the wraparound mortgage is secured by the property. And, like the bank, the seller is only interested in the portion of the mortgage he or she holds.

Imaginative financing of mortgages comes from awareness of the various ways to arrange them.

MORTGAGING A HOME VERSUS AN INVESTMENT PROPERTY

Before considering the many sources of mortgage money and various ways you can make financing work, let's clarify what we're using this money for. Specifically, do these techniques work for buying a home, investment property, or a piece of land? One of the myths about buying real estate is that you finance each property with a different type of loan. Nothing could be further from the truth.

■ *KEY POINT:* *Mortgage loans are basically the same for all property types.*

The tight money and high interest rates of just a few years ago brought forth some intricate financial devices. They were used not only by purchasers of income and commercial property but also by homebuyers. Financing an investment property is rarely different from financing a house. In many investment properties, even a multiunit apartment project, financing is conventional although several banks may participate as one to pool the necessary funds.

■ *KEY POINT:* *On large properties, several banks may combine their funds into one mortgage.*

Even in the purchase of a house, the seller, more often than not, is willing to give financial help to a responsible buyer.

■ *KEY POINT:* *Sellers are often willing to give financing.*

This book is not only about the many intricacies of conventional or creative financing. Its main thrust concerns the negotiations between buyer and lender that must take place to get a mortgage commitment. If you know which financial technique will benefit you and can present it in simple terms to the lender or seller, you have a greater chance of gaining favorable approval.

■ *KEY POINT:*   *Financing involves negotiating a particular technique.*

TERMS YOU SHOULD ALWAYS HAVE IN A MORTGAGE AGREEMENT

In buying a property, whether as a home or for investment, price and terms are intricately interwoven. For example, if you pay $100,000 for a property and the seller carries back a mortgage of $90,000 at two points below the going interest rate, you've gotten a bargain. In this case, the current interest rate is 11%, but you only pay 9% on the $90,000. This difference of 2% based on the $90,000 means that you are paying much less in overall cost for the property.

Any time you can negotiate a lower interest rate than the prevailing rate, it's the same as paying that much less for the property.

■ *KEY POINT:*   *Less interest means less overall cost.*

A major consideration in keeping your mortgage costs down is "points." These points are based on the amount of the mortgage; for example, three points are three percentage points of your mortgage. If you get an $80,000 mortgage, you will pay $2,400 as a fee for the privilege of securing the loan.

■ *CAUTION NOTE:*   *Percentage points are extra fees charged to you when you start a loan.*

Each bank may decide whether or not to charge points. It may do so either at the initiation of the mortgage or upon any prepayment. Several years from now when you may need to sell, you don't want the bank to charge you an extra 2% to 3%—

points based on the balance of the mortgage—as a fee for paying off the loan.

■ *CAUTION NOTE: Prepayment points may be charged on the balance at the time you pay off the loan.*

If a lender with whom you wish to do business does charge points on prepayment, insist on a time limit, after which the points will no longer be charged. For example, if the loan is held for four years, the four-point penalty will drop to two points, and then at six years no prepayment penalty will be charged.

■ *KEY POINT: Insist on time limits for the charging of prepayment points.*

What makes points particularly odious is that they are often charged for fixed-rate loans and not for ARMs. Doesn't that tell you that banks want to lend their money on variable-payment plans? The following chapters will provide more information on negotiating points downward.

■ *CAUTION NOTE: Points are more commonly charged with conventional fixed-rate loans.*

Lenders often wish to tie personal insurance—life and disability insurance—to the mortgage balance. Such insurance is often expensive, particularly if it is "whole life" not the "term" variety. However, as a borrower about to make a large financial commitment, you should assure that your family is protected with enough life and disability insurance. As an alternative to mortgage-tied policies (which are expensive gimmicks), you are better off reviewing your current coverage and updating policies.

Any time you can allow someone else to assume your mortgage in the future, you will get a distinct advantage. Several years from now, you may want to pass this assumable mortgage on to someone else.

■ *KEY POINT:* *If someone else can assume your mortgage, it may be an immense advantage in the future.*

Making a new loan assumable is more difficult to negotiate than points, but not impossible. Banks have lobbied for laws to stop loans from being assumed. In some states, banks are willing to allow a second party to assume payment on a loan, notably, if they have the right to judge the creditworthiness of the new borrower. The name of the first borrower often remains on the loan, however, in addition to the name of the new borrower.

■ *KEY POINT:* *Many loans can be assumed legally.*

Other terms and conditions vary with the mortgage. A conventional mortgage with a fixed rate of interest and period is straightforward in comparison with an adjustable plan. If you have an ARM or some variation (discussed in Chapter 8), such as charging payments, make sure no terms in your mortgage agreement penalize you beyond the normal principal and interest.

■ *KEY POINT:* *Limit changes to interest and principal only.*

Terms can vary as much as the many kinds and ways to arrange a mortgage. With a blanket mortgage, discussed in Chapter 4, you put additional property as security for the new loan. If it makes sense for you to arrange your loan this way, negotiate a time limit. For example, you don't want two properties pledged together for the full term of the mortgage. At some point, perhaps in as soon as three years, the value of the property you are buying will increase enough so the property pledged as security can be dropped from the blanket loan agreement.

■ *CAUTION NOTE:* *Negotiate time limits to release secured property from blanket loans.*

These are only some of the many terms you must negotiate to protect yourself. And, you can't rely on anyone besides yourself to negotiate the best deal for you. You can't expect the bank to look out for you. The real estate agent just wants the deal and rarely can do more than steer you to different banks. Your lawyer can help; however, he or she is more oriented toward preparing the deed and searching the title than arranging your mortgage. You are expected to negotiate the mortgage. Nobody is likely to give you more than advice. You have to talk to the bank.

■ *CAUTION NOTE: You are the best person to negotiate terms for your mortgage.*

Banks are not difficult to do business with. Most banks have reasonable guidelines; some are more flexible than others. Banks often differ on the terms they're willing to negotiate. And banks in one area may have similar but different policies from those in other areas.

■ *KEY POINT: Banks are easy to work with.*

All bankers may seem to get together on what they'll charge for interest. They really don't. It's illegal for them to set policy among themselves about what they charge or what they pay out to their depositors. Although this is good news for consumers, charges will still be similar because small banks borrow from larger banks, which in turn borrow from even more central banks.

■ *KEY POINT: Legally, banks cannot get together and set rates.*

More flexibility in banking practices comes in the terms and conditions under which money is lent out. Here is where you have the room to negotiate the most helpful mortgage.

WHEN TO TURN TO PROFESSIONALS

When you need advice, you can get some help from professionals. Even if you are buying a property on which the seller is going to give you back the mortgage, sit down with your neighborhood banker to find out what loans and terms might be available from that institution. This may help you in negotiating with the seller.

■ *KEY POINT: Preliminary contact with bankers helps in negotiating later.*

Bankers want to loan you money. That's their job—to act as salespeople for their bank. They have to get loans out the door. Many times, they're willing to help in negotiating around complex conditions offered by the bank. The disadvantage is that they may be prejudiced to the bank's position. True, their advice is often less than neutral, but talking to several bankers will give you an overall picture of the terms and conditions you can negotiate.

■ *KEY POINT: Valuable information comes from personal contact.*

Other professionals include local real estate agents. You may be using one in your purchase. His or her advice can be invaluable in negotiating a loan, particularly with a seller.

Again, if you must take the real estate agent's advice, do so with caution, particularly if he or she is involved in selling you the property in question. Otherwise, you may end up with undesirable mortgage terms. Agents negotiate mortgages all the time for many different buyers. They can provide invaluable advice on available loans and terms—all before you even visit the bank.

■ *KEY POINT: Real estate salespeople are savvy negotiators of mortgage terms and conditions.*

Your lawyer—always have a lawyer when buying any property—can help, particularly if you and the bank are stuck. Also, the negotiation of a loan from a seller needs to be written up into a formal document.

■ *KEY POINT:* *Your lawyer can help negotiate a difficult problem.*

There is a new form of professional counseling, whose practitioners are called real estate counselors or advisors. These people have experience in real estate, and for a fee, they will act as neutral advisors. They don't sell property but can help you with a specific problem such as having a property surveyed or deciding when to sell. They can also help you get a mortgage.

Instead of acting like an agent, who is pledged to the seller, real estate counselors work for you. They act on your behalf.

Since they do not receive a commission on the sale of the property, they work for a flat fee. This varies according to the kind of advice and the amount of time needed to help you. Fees can range anywhere from $50 to $150 for advice on negotiating a mortgage.

■ *KEY POINT:* *Real estate counselors work on your behalf in negotiating different types of mortgages.*

If you need someone locally, the real estate counselor may be the lead person. Compared with the other parties to a sale, his or her advice should be the most impartial.

In Chapter 4, we will examine the different sources from which you can get a mortgage.

DECIDING HOW MUCH YOU CAN AFFORD

Deciding how much you as a borrower can afford is one of the first steps in getting a mortgage. This chapter offers some guidelines to help you determine a comfortable range of afford-ability.

WHAT CAN YOU AFFORD?

How big a mortgage you can afford has a lot to do with how much you can spend on a house. Table 4.1 will help you decide how much house you can afford. It factors your income and a variety of interest rates. The table assumes a 10% cash down payment and monthly payments for mortgage, property taxes, and insurance that will equal 30 percent of your gross income.

Table 4.1 shows how much less you can afford for each rise in interest rate. For example, in the $50,000 income row, the differ-ence between paying a mortgage of 6% and paying one of 12% is more than $60,000 in the amount of house you can afford; in the $80,000 row, it is more than $100,000.

■ *CAUTION NOTE: Each rise in interest rate dramatically increases cost.*

SHOPPING FOR THE BEST RATES

Surprisingly, mortgage rates can vary widely, and as you can see in Table 4.1, interest rates can be critical in making it financially

Figures shown assume a 10% down payment and monthly mortgage payments that equal 30% of gross income. Property taxes and insurance equal 5%.

House Cost at 25-Year Fixed Rate

Taxes\Ins.	Income Range	Monthly Payment Available	6%	7%	8%	9%	10%	11%	12%
$1,000	$ 20,000	$ 416	$ 64,670	$ 58,953	$ 53,986	$ 49,651	$ 45,853	$ 42,512	$ 39,561
1,500	30,000	625	97,004	88,429	80,978	74,494	68,758	63,776	59,354
2,000	40,000	833	125,339	117,905	107,970	99,325	91,676	85,034	79,139
2,500	50,000	1,042	161,674	147,383	134,963	124,156	114,595	106,293	98,924
3,000	60,000	1,250	194,009	176,859	161,956	143,987	137,514	127,551	118,708
3,500	70,000	1,458	226,343	206,335	188,848	173,818	160,433	148,810	138,493
4,000	80,000	1,667	258,679	235,812	215,941	198,649	183,352	170,068	158,278
4,500	90,000	1,875	291,013	265,288	242,933	223,480	206,271	191,327	178,063
5,000	100,000	2,083	323,347	294,764	269,926	248,331	229,190	212,585	197,847

Table 4.1. How much can you afford?

possible for you to pay a mortgage. For example, payments on an 8.5%, $90,000, 25-year fixed-rate loan are $724 a month, compared with $786, or almost $800, for the same loan at 9.5%.

A 6% ARM would mean initial payments of $580 a month, but inevitably these ARM payments will rise in the future. As you can see in Table 4.2, which shows monthly payments for each $1,000 borrowed, payments climb at each higher interest rate.

Look down the interest rate column in Table 4.2 for the rate at which you wish to calculate the monthly payment, and across to the right for the mortgage term columns, 15 through 30 years. The amount shown is the monthly payment for each

Interest rate	Monthly Payments per $1,000 Borrowed			
	15 years	20 years	25 years	30 years
6.00	$ 8.44	$ 7.16	$ 6.44	$ 6.00
6.25	8.57	7.31	6.60	6.16
6.50	8.71	7.46	6.75	6.32
6.75	8.85	7.60	6.91	6.49
7.00	8.99	7.75	7.07	6.65
7.25	9.13	7.90	7.23	6.82
7.50	9.27	8.06	7.39	6.99
7.75	9.41	8.21	7.55	7.16
8.00	9.56	8.36	7.79	7.34
8.25	9.70	8.52	7.89	7.51
8.50	9.85	8.68	8.06	7.69
8.75	9.99	8.84	8.22	7.87
9.00	10.14	9.00	8.39	8.05
9.25	10.29	9.16	8.56	8.23
9.50	10.44	9.32	8.74	8.41
9.75	10.59	9.49	8.91	8.59
10.00	10.75	9.65	9.09	8.78
10.25	10.90	9.82	9.26	8.97
10.50	11.06	9.98	9.44	9.15
10.75	11.21	10.15	9.62	9.34
11.00	11.37	10.32	9.80	9.53
11.25	11.53	10.49	9.98	9.72
11.50	11.69	10.66	10.16	9.91
11.75	11.85	10.84	10.35	10.10
12.00	12.01	11.01	10.53	10.29

Table 4.2. Payment table.

$1,000 borrowed. To find the monthly payment for a particular loan, simply divide that amount by 1,000 and multiply the result by the payment per $1,000. For example, if you need to borrow $85,000 for 25 years at 9.5%, go across the 9.5% row to the 25-year column; the payment shown is $8.74 per $1,000. Your monthly payment, then, would be $743, or 8.74 times 85.

PRIVATE AND PUBLIC LOAN GUIDELINES

It is essential to understand how lenders will check your loan application. Knowing what they are looking for allows you to match your needs to theirs. Table 4.2 uses 30% for interest and principal, property taxes, and insurance. This is an average figure that measures your borrowing power as a ratio of housing expenses to your gross household income.

■ *KEY POINT: Many lenders use 30% as a basic expense guideline.*

The Federal National Mortgage Association (Fannie Mae; FNMA) uses the figures of 28% and 36%; specifically, the monthly mortgage interest and principal payments, plus property taxes and homeowner's insurance, should total no more than 28% of your gross monthly income. Additionally, your monthly house payments plus other long-term debts, such as automobile or student loans, should total no more than 36% of your gross income.

■ *CAUTION NOTE: Fannie Mae uses 28% as a limit for property expenses.*

Many banks follow these Fannie Mae guidelines, as they often wish to repackage a group of loans and resell them. Income defined by Fannie Mae is the work you have been doing for a year or longer, not the extra income you are getting from a part-time job you started last month. Even such extra income as bonuses, commissions, and overtime must be averaged for at least two years to be considered wages. Child-support payments and alimony are only considered income if the payments will continue at least three years into the future.

■ *CAUTION NOTE:* *Lenders often wish to sell loans that meet Fannie Mae guidelines.*

To qualify for adjustable-rate mortgages, where you might face steep rate hikes in the future, you must meet even stricter requirements. If your ARM starts with a low initial rate, such as 6% with a 2% maximum increase per year, capping out at 5% (over the term of the mortgage), Fannie Mae, and in turn your lender, may analyze this mortgage based on an 8% or 9% rate.

If you wish to make a down payment of less than 10% of the purchase price, Fannie Mae and your bank are likely to look at a stricter ratio of housing expense to income, such as 25% and 30%. This means that for a $91,000 loan on a $100,000 house, your payments cannot be more than one-quarter of your long-term debt, no more than 33% of income.

These are not strict guidelines. Even Fannie Mae treats every mortgage on its own merits. Many factors can tip the scales one way or another; the most important factors on gaining a mortgage can be a stable credit history, large down payment, and assets equal to at least three months of mortgage payments in reserve. Thus, their 28% guideline can reach 30% or more.

■ *CAUTION NOTE:* *Fannie Mae guidelines are usually stricter than individual bank policies.*

A rough guideline for you is that monthly loan payments, including insurance and taxes, should equal 30% or less of your gross household income. Many banks, such as those that sell their mortgages through the Fannie Mae system, have a guideline of 28% or less. However, the rise in interest rates and overall housing costs has caused many lenders, as well as borrowers, to realize that they must allot more for monthly housing costs than was once considered acceptable.

MAKING THE MOST OF YOUR BORROWING POWER

Start by analyzing your monthly expenses. If your long-term, basic expenses exceed 35% of your income, consider selling some assets, such as stocks or mutual fund shares, to pay off some of this debt. As with the down payment, seek help from family, relatives, or friends in cleaning up these debts.

■ *KEY POINT:* *Keep long-term debts to a reasonable limit.*

Frequently, when you offer to make a larger down payment and bring some of your expenses up to date, the lender will demand written proof that any money you receive is a gift, not a disguised loan. Remember, the lender's key concern is that you, without help from outside sources, can meet the new financial needs of owning a property.

■ *CAUTION NOTE:* *Sometimes, particularly if you put down a minimal down payment, the lender requires unborrowed money.*

WILL SHORT- OR LONG-TERM WORK BEST FOR YOU?

All mortgages, whether from a bank or seller, whether conventional or creative, have a stated length of time over which payments are made to satisfy the debt. Once a standard mortgage was 20 to 25 years. In recent years, mortgages have crept up to 30 years or more. Many people have opted for these long-term mortgages as they spread the loan out over more years, making the payments slightly less.

■ *KEY POINT:* *Long-term payment schedules mean lower payments.*

However, at some point you will want to pay off the principal balance on the loan. As you saw in Chapter 1, the amount of the monthly payment reducing the overall balance, or principal, does not become a significant portion of the monthly payment until the later stages of the mortgage. Many investors look at income property on the basis that it will generate enough cash to meet the requirements of shorter payoff. They plan on holding their property awhile and don't want to pay off the enormous amount of interest due over a 30-year term. They seek to pay off a 15- or even a 12-year loan.

■ *CAUTION NOTE: More interest is paid for a long-term loan.*

■ *KEY POINT: Principal is paid off more quickly with a short-term loan.*

The same is true if you buy a house. If you can afford the higher payments of a 15- or 20-year mortgage, you will bring down your indebtedness much more rapidly than with a longer loan.

Your monthly payment is higher, but as Table 4.3 shows, the differences between the payments in a 30-year and 20-year loan are not as extensive as you might think. And look at how much less interest you pay over the whole term. The interest paid over the period of the loan is much less when the mortgage is for a shorter term.

There can be a dramatic difference in the reduction of principal balance in the short-term mortgage. By the 13th year of the 15-year mortgage, you would have only a remaining balance of about 22%. After the 13th year of the 30-year loan, more than 79% of the principal balance remains. In fact, not until the 24th year in the 30-year loan would you have paid off more than 50% of the original loan—more than 9 years after you would have completed the loan under the 15-year plan.

This does not mean that long-term mortgages are bad for you. Most property, whether a home or investment, is not held for the duration of the loan. The average family moves every four to five years, their requirements constantly changing. Investment properties are usually held for longer periods.

■ *KEY POINT: The average holding period for residential property is less than five years.*

$75,000 mortgage for 30 years at 9% compared with the same loan amount and percentage for 15 years.

Monthly payments: 15-year loan = $760.70
                    30-year loan = $603.47

Remaining balance as a percentage of original loan amount

| Age of Loan | Original Term | |
	15 years	30 years
1	97	99
2	93	99
3	89	98
4	85	97
5	80	96
7	69	94
9	56	91
11	41	88
13	22	84
15	0	79

Table 4.3.   Long-term versus short-term mortgage.

Your situation is unique. The money you have available for payments must set the guidelines whether you opt for a short- or long-term mortgage.

■ *KEY POINT: The money for payments often decides the length of term of the mortgage.*

ADJUSTING YOUR DOWN PAYMENT

Varying your own down payment to meet your needs is one way to keep your monthly payments in line with what you can afford. If you have the cash or have equity in an existing home, you can keep your mortgage loan at a minimum by making as high a down payment as possible on your new property.

At 8.5% for 20 years, the difference between a $90,000 loan and a $75,000 loan is $131 per month. This is very helpful if you are buying for the second or third time and have equity built up in a previous property.

■ *KEY POINT: A larger down payment means less monthly cost.*

THE PROBLEM OF A LOW DOWN PAYMENT

Often the biggest obstacle facing first-time homebuyers today is not getting a mortgage but getting a down payment together. Occasionally, you can put down as little as 5% of the purchase price, but closer to 20% is common.

You should make sure that your down payment won't unduly restrict your other financial needs. However, it also must be large enough to keep down the amount of mortgage money you need. As you can see in Table 4.1, monthly mortgage payments can exceed $1,000 a month in a loan approaching $125,000 at 9%. Therefore, the more you can put down, the less you must borrow and the lower your monthly payments will be.

■ *CAUTION NOTE: A low down payment causes high monthly mortgage payments and restricts other needy purchases.*

Many government-backed FHA loans for low- and middle-income homebuyers, and VA loans for veterans, allow homebuyers to make no down payment or a very low one. But putting as much down as possible means you not only secure your chances at getting a loan, but you reduce the amount of mortgage money you will need to borrow.

However, for those who don't have the equity from one house to put into the purchase of a new one, making the mortgage payments is easier than coming up with a big lump sum of cash for the down payment, points, and other closing costs.

HOW TO SAVE FOR THE DOWN PAYMENT

Sometimes, setting money aside for the down payment is a battle. Here are some ways to get a hold on your finances. First, faithfully log every dollar spent on a monthly chart that records all payments and income in detail. Now look for expenses that seem out of line. You may be spending far more than necessary on entertainment or lawn care. Or your grocery bill may have too much for household supplies in comparison with the amount you spend for food. You may see that you are drawing too frequently for cash. Or using your credit cards excessively.

Next you must make buying your dream house a top priority. Decide how much you are going to put in a savings account every month. Forgo extras such as vacations, second car, or new computer. If you are renting, do it inexpensively until you save your down payment.

The key is self-control. Tight discipline to a savings plan makes it less likely to splurge on unnecessary expenses. Do your best to put a specific sum into your account every month.

■ *KEY POINT:* *Essential to saving a down payment is control over expenses.*

DOWN PAYMENT HELP FROM PARENTS

Select banks allow parents (and sometimes employers) to come to the help of their children in unusual ways. They offer 100% financing if a parent places a specific percentage of the purchase price—10% to 20%—in their bank as a certificate of deposit. Some banks even accept stock or mutual funds.

Your parent, as sponsor of the investment, still gets to keep all dividend and interest payments. Stock cannot be part of an Individual Retirement Account (IRA). It must be maintained in more than the amount of the down payment. If you meet these requirements the bank lends 100% of market value.

■ *KEY POINT:* *Parents can put up stock or CD equity to assure down payment.*

With points and closing costs on mortgages typically totalling 5% of the home's purchase price, you should make sure

you understand what if any additional fees this option may en-
tail. An application fee of as much as $300 may be charged. As
sponsors, your parents may be charged an additional 2% to 3%
of the guarantee amount annually, although this fee may end
when the principal amount is reduced 25% to 30%.

There may be other drawbacks besides the added closing
costs in programs of this nature. The lender is likely to require
mortgage insurance, which could amount to $1/2$% of the outstanding loan amount annually. Banks that offer this program
usually limit the amount of the purchase price to under
$200,000.

■ *CAUTION NOTE: Additional costs result from down payment programs.*

A better strategy may be to borrow all or a portion—5% to
10%—of the down payment from your parents. The extra closing fees, mortgage insurance, and annual sponsorship charge
may make a parental loan the less costly route.

■ *KEY POINT: Borrowing direct from parents costs less.*

Programs like this show that some lenders have made it easier for parents to help with their children's down payment. By
accepting a guarantee from parents instead of cash, lenders go
on record they are no longer concerned whether down payment
money comes from the borrowers or their parents. This attitude
varies from bank to bank. Many lenders still insist that buyers
contribute some personal funds.

The government also encourages parents to aid with down
payments. Fannie Mae sets lending standards for the loans it
buys back. Their Community Home Buyer's Program lets first-
time buyers with household earnings below 115% of median
area income have an outsider, usually a parent or employer,
contribute two-fifths of the 5% minimum needed for the down
payment.

Before, anyone using Fannie Mae's "5% down" program had
to prove they could put down the full amount themselves.

Current thought is that unless this restriction is eased, many might be unable to buy a home.

MORTGAGE INSURANCE

A stipulation regularly required by the lender for borrowers putting down less than 20% is that they buy private mortgage insurance, usually available through the lender. This guarantees the loan until the equity in your home equals 20% of the fair market value. Federal mortgage insurance is included in FHA and VA loans.

■ *KEY POINT:* *Mortgage insurance is usually required for minimal down payments.*

This mortgage insurance, which varies between 0.5% and 1.5% at the closing, adds $20 to $35 to the monthly payment on average; it becomes more expensive the smaller your down payment gets.

Some lending institutions want to charge more points if you make a minimal down payment, so beg or borrow from your friends and family to put down at least 15%, if not 20%. By doing so, you reduce the number of points needed and drop private mortgage insurance, which makes quick approval of your mortgage application easier. Banks always have to look more closely at deals where the purchasing of property is made with less than 20% down. They may take extra time to scrutinize credit and property value, delaying a decision on your mortgage application.

■ *CAUTION NOTE:* *A low down payment can often delay a mortgage application because of scrutiny of credit and property.*

HOW POINTS AFFECT AFFORDABILITY

As previously discussed, points are taken out when you get your loan. Each point equals 1% of the loan, which can be costly and become a determining factor in which loan you choose. For example, which $100,000 loan would you choose: 10% with three points, that is, $3,000, or 10.25% with 1.5 points, or $1,500?

At first glance, it may appear that paying the extra point and a half to get the lower interest rate is a superior deal. If you plan to stay in the property for only a few years, however, it will take a lot of extra monthly payments to equal the $1,500 cost of additional points. But, if you need to lessen monthly payments to qualify for a mortgage, consider paying all three points up front to get the lower rate.

■ *CAUTION NOTE: Points, like other closing costs, take years to pay back.*

HOW VARIABLE RATES PLAY HAVOC WITH YOUR BUDGET

One of the many reasons you must be careful in choosing an ARM is that you are then subject to the ups and downs of interest rates, and the ups can raise havoc with your monthly budget. As you can see in Table 4.1, a rise of two points in interest over the course of the year can make astronomical jumps in your monthly mortgage payment. In a variable-rate loan, what starts as 6% or 6.5% can often be a point and a half or two points higher within a year. Possibly, in three or four years, the increase will cap out 4% or 5% higher, depending on the specific terms of your loan.

■ *CAUTION NOTE: A variable rate sliding upward can cause a considerable rise in your monthly payment.*

It is true, however, that the uncertainty of higher rates in the future is somewhat balanced out by lower initial rates that give you some rate hike protection in the early years. You just have to be prepared to pay higher rates in the future. Further, if you are planning on being in the house for a short period, an adjustable rate may be the wisest course.

■ *KEY POINT:* *A higher rate in the future is often balanced by a lower initial rate.*

These are comparisons you must make with the mortgages available to you in your local marketplace. Compare, for example, a 9%, fixed-rate mortgage; a one-year ARM at 5.5% with a 2% interest rate cap in any given year and a 5% cap over the life of the loan; and a three-year ARM at 8% with the same 2% to 5% caps. In the worst situation, the one-year ARM will rise to 7.5% after year one, to 9.5% after year two (making it more expensive than the fixed-rate mortgage), and to 10.5%—the maximum allowed—in the next year. The three-year ARM, in contrast, isn't adjusted for the extra two percentage points to 10% until after year three. You only beat the fixed-rate loan on a short period on both, and only for an extra year on the three-year ARM (see Table 4.4).

Underlying this whole discussion, particularly about adjustable-rate loans, is that it is fruitless to predict where these loans are going, whether they will rise or fall. What you must hope for, if you choose an ARM, is that rates will remain stable and that your initial lower ARM rate will stay low.

■ *CAUTION NOTE:* *Caution is required for ARMs because of the unpredictable nature of varying interest rates.*

Year	Fixed-Rate Mortgage (%)	One-Year ARM (%)	Three-Year ARM (%)
1	9	5½	6½
2	9	7½	6½
3	9	9½	8½
4	9	10½	10½
		(maximum allowed)	

Table 4.4. Worst-case mortgage comparison.

One recommendation is to consider convertible ARMs, which allow you to switch from an adjustable-rate to a fixed-rate mortgage. At similar cost, it is wise to choose the convertible ARM in case interest rates skyrocket. However, there are fees for converting to a fixed-rate loan, so you must analyze the final financial impact before deciding to make the change.

■ *KEY POINT: Consider an ARM that allows conversion to a conventional loan.*

The next chapter will explain how to choose the right mortgage plan.

CHOOSING THE 5 RIGHT MORTGAGE

The common problem in financing a real estate purchase is not finding the mortgage but choosing the best mortgage among several competing choices. Unlike a decade ago, many lenders and banking institutions are now competing for your business. Interest rates, the monthly payments you can afford, the term in which the loan will be negotiated, and the points to originate a loan, as well as the prepayment points for paying off a loan before its maturity, are among the several factors you need to consider in choosing the right loan.

■ *KEY POINT:* *Many lenders compete for your business.*

The key is to work within your financial bounds, that is, what you can afford now and in the future. For many of us, that means squeezing into a loan in the beginning. It is even stretching our ability to make monthly payments, so in the future, with possible rising income, we can settle in comfortably to our payment schedule.

■ *KEY POINT:* *Sometimes, we must expect future income to meet our loan schedule.*

If you lack cash to put down on a property and have to make a minimal down payment, you will increase the amount of money you pay monthly. You must make up that difference in the amount of income you receive. If you have owned a house before or have some cash, or if you can get help from your family to make a larger down payment, your mortgage and therefore your monthly payments will not be as high and may fit better into your financial structure.

■ *KEY POINT: A higher down payment means a smaller mortgage and thus smaller monthly payments.*

Most people today will still choose a conventional, self-amortizing mortgage having a fixed rate of interest over a 25- or 30-year term, with 10% or 15% down and constant, equal monthly payments. You will want to compare the terms of this conventional mortgage with many of the other loans you consider, such as adjustable-rate mortgages.

■ *KEY POINT: Most borrowers opt for a steady rate, self-amortizing, conventional loan that requires a modest amount down.*

As you have seen in this book, the rates for some variable-interest loans start below the average conventional rate but eventually may rise to a higher percentage than the fixed rate.

■ *CAUTION NOTE: Avoid a variable rate that could escalate unreasonably.*

SHOPPING FOR A MORTGAGE

Here are some major points to consider in choosing among available mortgage alternatives.

Type of Loan: Fixed Rate or Adjustable?

Should you get a fixed-rate or an adjustable-rate mortgage? Certainty comes with a fixed-rate loan because you pay the same amount to your lender every month. With the adjustable-rate mortgage, although the interest rate can initially be lower, it can rise and fall during the term of the mortgage. It normally starts at a lower rate, such as $1^1/_2$ to $2^1/_2$ points below that for fixed mortgages. It does have limits, such as no more than a 2-point rise over the course of a year, or 5 or 6 percentage points over the term of the mortgage. Even one or two percentage points on a mortgage can affect your monthly payments.

■ *CAUTION NOTE: Make sure adjustable loans contain limits on rate rises.*

ARMs are attractive if you plan to sell a house in three or four years: That way you are not likely to get stuck with the 2% or 4% increase in your monthly payments that will probably be added on in a few years. The changes will depend a lot on the difference between the starting interest rate within an ARM and what is being charged for a conventional loan. If an adjustable-rate mortgage is $2^1/2$ or 3 points lower than a fixed-rate mortgage, it is wise for you to consider this. You can often convert this loan to a fixed-rate loan in the future, even if you have to go to another lending institution.

■ *KEY POINT: With an ARM, there is always the chance of future conversion or renegotiation.*

In deciding on an ARM loan, you must consider your expectations for future income: Will it rise dramatically within a few years? If you are in a low budget but in a job where your income and position will advance, the lower rate now may be something to consider. If you are on a more fixed income and don't see any excess cash in the future, now may be the time for you to lock in that fixed rate.

Today's comparatively low rates are so reasonable that it may be wiser to select a predictable payment rather than an initially lower monthly payment. On the other hand, with the rate on one-year ARM hovering at 5% to 6%, you could get a $110,000 ARM now instead of a $100,000 fixed-rate loan. If you wish to build up equity fast, you must also consider the popular 15-year, fixed-rate loan; its payments, however, are 20% to 25% higher than those for a 30-year loan. Rates on 1-year ARMs change annually and often follow 1-year Treasury securities.

A Balloon Option?

One way to afford more house is to consider a balloon mortgage. The rate is fixed as is the monthly payment if the loan were paid over a set number of years, usually 25 to 30 years. At the end of 5 or 7 years, however, the remaining principal comes due or must be refinanced. Although this "two-step" loan is usually at a slightly more costly rate, from the bank's point of view it involves less risk. At the end of the 5 or 7 years, you are automatically offered a new rate determined by market conditions. This new rate is usually capped at 5% or 6% above the original.

The balloon option is one to consider if you must move within a few years.

■ *KEY POINT:* *The balloon mortgage is often a good choice when you intend to keep the property for only a brief time.*

Term of Loan: Short or Long?

Short-term loans have been desirable in recent years as moderate rates have allowed borrowers to afford the payments demanded by a more rapid payoff schedule. The primary impetus, then, is to reduce the amount of interest paid out over the life of the mortgage or to pay off the loan near or before retirement.

■ *KEY POINT:* *Short-term loans reduce interest paid.*

An obvious advantage is the sizable amount of money you can save in interest over the term of the mortgage. For example, an $80,000 loan with an 8.5%, 25-year term has monthly payments of $644; with an 8%, 15-year loan (you usually get a slightly lower interest rate for choosing a shorter-term loan), the payment is $765 a month.

Though it costs $121 more a month, total payments on the shorter loan would be $55,500 less over the life of the loan, compared with the 25-year term. If you are keeping the house over the term of its loan, you can see that the short term might be wise. Even if you sell within a few years, the 15-year loan has paid off equity at a more rapid rate. Over the first 6 years, for example, you would have paid an extra $8,712 on the 15-year mortgage, but would have amassed $14,027 more equity (principal paid off) than with the 25-year loan.

■ *KEY POINT: Short-term loans mean rapid principal layoff.*

In negotiating a short-term loan to save interest expense, you must consider what the money spent on the higher payments can earn elsewhere. Payments are about 20% to 25% lower on a 30-year loan than on a 15-year loan. That in itself is a large difference, but consider what other opportunities you can pursue with that extra money over the course of the loan. For example, the difference of $121 in the monthly payment illustrated in the preceding example, if invested at 10% over 6 years, would grow to $11,871—comparable but still less than the savings in principal payoff.

■ *CAUTION NOTE: Rapid principal payoff in a short-term loan must be balanced against growth earned by your money elsewhere.*

Granted, some of us need the discipline of a forced savings plan. However, if you took the amount you saved each month on the lower payments of the long-term loan and put it into an investment that yielded more than the interest on your mortgage, you could have considerably more money over the full term of the mortgage. Plus, you would have money at your immediate disposal should you need it for a major expenditure.

In conclusion, it is often hard to say whether a 15- or 20-year loan is better than a 25- or 30-year loan. With a short-term loan, you often can negotiate a lower interest rate. Sometimes, however, you can make a wiser investment than the cost of your mortgage with the extra monthly money this loan requires. A 15-year, $75,000 mortgage at an average rate of 8% costs about $682 a month versus $603 for the 30-year, 9% loan—a difference of about 12% in higher monthly costs. With the short-term loan, however, the rate may be one-half to a full point less than on the long-term mortgage. And for the length of the term, you will cut your interest charges about in half.

■ *KEY POINT:* *The decision on short or long term is often one of personal preference.*

You also have to remember that mortgage interest is tax-deductible. The extra interest you pay on a long-term loan is at least deductible, if somewhat diminished, under the lower tax rate of the new tax code.

With a short-term loan, shelling out more dollars but paying less interest swells your monthly costs. This is in contrast to the lower payments of the 30-year loan that may allow you to afford a larger and more suitable home. If you take out the short-term mortgage, you are locked into higher payments and committed to an investment yielding whatever that mortgage rate is. As other opportunities at higher rates come your way over the years, you may not have this extra money to invest.

■ *KEY POINT:* *The lower payments of a long-term loan may allow you to afford a larger home.*

For those who choose longer payment plans, there is always the opportunity of accelerating payments. You can even add a set amount to each monthly payment, almost creating your own mortgage plan, and thus effectively shorten the term of your long-term loan. You could also send your lender a lump-sum amount at the end of the year, should you come into extra money. These additional monies are applied against the principal, thereby shortening the term of the loan and decreasing the amount of interest you will pay.

■ *KEY POINT:* *Most mortgage balances can be brought down with extra payments made at your convenience.*

The goal is, if you have something better to do with your extra money—and have the proper discipline—you can save at a higher rate of interest than your present mortgage interest rate. Overall, the better investment opportunity is the one with the higher interest. This doesn't mean that choosing the shorter term may not be helpful for you. It depends on what your income is, how long you intend to live in the home, and whether you are a wise investor. There are advantages to both short-term and long-term loans.

■ *CAUTION NOTE: Discipline is needed to make regular payments to an investment plan designed to take advantage of lower mortgage payments.*

If alternative rates of investment are less than the interest rate on your mortgage, you may be wise to invest at the rate of your mortgage, specifically by paying off a portion of your mortgage balance. In this way, you are decreasing a committed higher rate instead of earning less at a lower rate. You can do this by adding to your monthly payments or making lump-sum payments against the outstanding balance.

■ *KEY POINT: Invest at your rate of mortgage by making extra payments.*

Cost of Property: Large or Small Mortgage?

Obvious, but often unstated, is that the cost of the house determines, to a large degree, the size of the mortgage needed to finance it. Whether you are putting down a minimum of 5% or a larger 20% to 30%, the size of the mortgage does not trail far behind the purchase price.

■ *KEY POINT: Purchase in the range you can afford.*

Rate of Interest

When you read in the paper about mortgage rates rising and falling, it may seem as if they all move in a concerted mass. In general, within regions throughout the country, rates do tend to move in lockstep, as they are often controlled by national financial policy.

However, the rates offered by banks in your local area can often vary a percentage point, so it is wise to shop around. Perhaps your local newspaper publishes weekly mortgage comparisons. Your agent can keep you informed, and there are services that offer research on current mortgage costs.

■ *KEY POINT: Shop local lenders for the best interest rate.*

There is often a connection between interest rates and prices of real estate. In some "hot" regions, people don't care about price, as long as they can find favorable financing, especially at rates that look like bargains. Conversely, a higher interest rate often translates into lower property prices. Real estate prices also may vary with the availability or scarcity of mortgage money. This is a helpful point if, with your mortgage proposal, you can edge out fellow mortgage seekers for that scarce money and thus can buy at a comparatively lower price. Current conditions in both the real estate and mortgage markets affect the lender's willingness to negotiate on rates.

A variety of mortgages and rates are available to you at any one time. The rates in Table 5.1 are averages from recent years. You will have to check your local lending institutions for the precise rates being charged at any given time.

The table shows the differences between rates for various types of loans, as well as the points and amount of interest charged, based on a loan of $80,000. Down payments range between 5% and 30%, with fewer points paid with the higher down payments.

COMPARING LOANS

No single mortgage format is ideal for all borrowers. You need to choose the financial strategy that works for you. To make your decision easier, look at the amount of money you have for a down payment and your income level. Certainly, if you have plenty of money for a down payment and are married with a large income, you can afford most homes on the market.

Most people, however, particularly those negotiating a mortgage for their first property, have to squeeze into the property they can afford. They have to reduce the down payment requirement and skirt the edge of 28% to 30% of their gross annual income in calculating affordable mortgage payments and insurance and taxes.

Many varieties of mortgage exist and because of people's varied requirements, that is a boon. Two factors of particular interest to most people are interest rate (for example, variable interest on the adjustable-rate mortgages) and the term on which the loan is based.

■ *KEY POINT: You can choose among many varieties of mortgage format.*

Too many people automatically select the 30-year mortgage. As you can see from Table 5.1, a 30-year mortgage pays more interest than does a 15- or 20-year mortgage. People who think they are going to move within 4 or 5 years may not care about the term. If they don't pay off much principal, they will increase their equity, simply because the value of the property will increase. The decision on this factor depends on whether you will be staying in your new home or moving on in a few years.

■ *KEY POINT: Staying in a property for only a few years affects the choice of mortgage.*

If you are buying to settle down in an area, you may very well want to look at the 15- or 20-year mortgage with an eye to lessen your overall interest. You can also look at the short-term mortgage as an enforced savings plan, in that you are paying more per month, but in 15 or 20 years you can have a mortgage-burning party. So reducing the term to lower overall interest costs or reducing or extending monthly payments, making a lower or higher down payment, and negotiating

Type	Rate (%)	Minimum Down (%)	Recommended Down (%)	Points (%)	Monthly Payment ($)	Total Interest Cost ($)
30-year fixed	8–10	5	20	0–5	587–702	131,326–172,735
Remarks: Popular with first-time borrowers. Higher interest payments made over longer term. Fixed rate stabilizes interest.						
25-year fixed	7.5–9.5	5	20	0–4	591–699	97,350–129,684
Remarks: Fixed rate offers protection from increases. Slightly lower rate means less interest paid but higher monthly payment.						
20-year fixed	7.5–9.5	5	20	0–4	644–745	74,675–98,972
Remarks: Best recommendation during period of lower rates. Balanced in interest paid and length of term.						
15-year fixed	7–9	5	20	0–4	719–811	41,096–53,541
Remarks: Shortest term generally available. Highest payments but less interest paid overall.						
Minimal credit (20-year)	8.5–11	20	20	2–6	694–826	86,621–118,181
Remarks: Higher interest rate and more down for low-credit borrower. Higher payments and points result.						
Strong credit High Down (25-year)	7–9	25	30	1–3	565–671	89,628–121,404
Remarks: More down means lower interest rate and points.						
Bimonthly payment	8.25–9.5	5	20	1–3	631–699	109,228–129,684
Remarks: 26 payments per year. Excellent loan for negotiating low rate and points. Less interest over term. Extra payments require high income.						

7-year balloon (20-year)	7.5–9.5	5	20	1–4	644–745	38,239–49,305 (after 7 years)

Remarks: Lower payments and rate, but payoff in short term will require selling or refinancing. Possibly interest only.

10-year balloon (20-year)	7.5–9.5	5	20	1–4	644–745	51,631–67,114 (after 10 years)

Remarks: Same as 7-year balloon but longer time to negotiate payoff.

1-year adjustable (25-year)	5–7	5	20	0–3.5	468–591	60,302–97,360

Remarks: Lower promotional rate and possibly no points going in, but subject to uncertainty of future rate increases, particularly after first year.

3-year adjustable (25-year)	6–8.5	5	20	1–3	515–644	74,633–113,256

Remarks: As with one-year adjustable, lower beginning rate and points. With both, negotiate caps on yearly and life-of-loan interest rises. Good loans in higher interest periods for those who plan to sell in a short time.

Table 5.1. Mortgage market guide. (Based on mortgage principal of $80,000.)

points or interest rates, are all alternatives that can make the terms of a mortgage more suitable for you.

Not all banks offer every alternative discussed in this book. In fact, many of the new techniques that you read about in monthly periodicals never become a reality in local mortgage markets, where the choices must be made. However, the basic conventional loans—fixed-rate, adjustable-rate and fixed-rate loans with balloon payments, and convertible loans—are available at most lending institutions.

The right loan for you is the one that meets your particular needs and circumstances, allowing you to purchase the property. That is the key: to get a property you can afford. The loan is merely a financial tool with which you can purchase real estate. It is there to help you make up the difference between the down payment you can comfortably put down and the purchase price of the property.

■ *KEY POINT: A mortgage loan is merely a financial tool to purchase property, which you structure to pay back in a way that most logically meets your needs.*

DECIDING WHICH LOAN IS BEST

Choosing between the two main types of loan, the fixed-rate and the ARM, at first appears confusing. Rates for both are at historic lows. Those who have negotiated ARMs in the past few years have recently considered "converting" back to a fixed rate. The decision of which kind of mortgage often rests on how long you are going to stay at your new location. Or, if refinancing, how many more years you will stay. Simply stated, if you're planning a move in the next few years, an ARM may suit you well. If you're there for the long haul, you may opt for the fixed rate.

Since most ARMs are convertible to fixed rates, costs related to closing the changeover are minimal. If you desire a new mortgage, points and other costs may push this price up to several thousand dollars.

As you can see, an ARM that starts at 2% less than the equivalent 25- or 30-year fixed rate will cost you less over the first 3 to 4 years, even if rates rise appreciably.

An analogy shows the enticement of the adjustable rate. Monthly payments on a $120,000, 25-year mortgage at 8.5% would be $966; payments on a 5.75% one-year ARM would be $755 the first year. If the ARM's rate rose the maximum two percentage points a year for the next three years, you would save over that time $2,006 with the ARM. However, by the end of the 4th year, when your rate would be 11.75% (6% maximum rise), you would have paid out a total of $47,661, $1,293 more than for the fixed-rate loan.

■ *CAUTION NOTE: A beguilingly low ARM rate can hide a potentially higher cost.*

Whether rates will go up or down is a gamble. What you can do to make a reasoned decision is judge the length of time you plan to remain in the home. If you're buying for the first time and plan to trade up when the economy improves, an ARM might make good sense. In recent years of interest rates trending downward, such mortgages certainly have saved borrowers money. However, as rates may inevitably start cycling up again, the long-term loan may appear the astute choice.

Most new buyers in today's low-interest environment opt for the security of an unchanging monthly payment. While fixed rate mortgages offer control, however, they don't give you the optimal deal. If you plan on only staying a few years, your cost is less with an ARM. To decide on this fixed or floating rate, do some math. Take the number of years you plan to spend in your home and plot out the cost of each type of mortgage year by year, just as in the preceding example.

You may wish to relieve the dread of yearly adjustments by shopping for a long-term ARM—a 3- or 5-year ARM. Although the initial rate is higher than the one-year loan, the savings within a few years can be significant. And the extra time gives you a measure of safety over a rapid increase. In the same example, a 3-year ARM might be at 7.5% interest, which would cost $887 per month. Total payments after three years would be $2,842 less than with the 8.5% fixed-rate mortgage. They'd even be $836 less than you'd pay on the 1-year ARM, presuming maximum annual rate rises.

■ *KEY POINT: Consider long-term ARMs for more financial control.*

KNOW WHICH INDEX CONTROLS THE ARM

A question you always should ask lenders is which index they use to peg their ARMs. Many are connected to the rate on Treasury securities of the equivalent term. For example, a 1-year ARM will be based on the 1-year Treasury, or "T" bill, rate; a 3-year ARM, on the 3-year note.

Other indexes are used. Another common index is the "Eleventh District" cost of funds. Started by the Federal Home Loan Bank Board in the southwestern United States, the Eleventh District index is less volatile than Treasury rates. These rates tend to move up more slowly when interest rates rise and to drop more slowly when they fall.

Lenders look at these indexes 45 to 60 days before your loan's anniversary date and set your new rate accordingly. However, knowing which benchmark guides a bank's ARM can save costly mistakes.

■ *CAUTION NOTE: Judge the stability of the ARM index.*

GUIDELINES FOR COMPARING LOANS

Here are some guidelines you can use to compare different loans.

How Much Down Payment Must You Put Down?

The larger the mortgage you have, the higher your monthly payment is likely to be. The interest rate will be lower for a loan in which you can put at least 20% down.

Occasionally, banks will even give you a special deal if you can put 30% down. Unless you have owned a property before or have spent years saving money, you probably can't put a huge amount of money down. In putting down a small amount—5% or 10%—you need to look at the terms of the mortgage and structure them so you can afford your payments.

Is the Interest Rate Fixed or Variable?

Will the rate be fixed or will it change during the term of the loan, thereby affecting your monthly payments? Are these changes scheduled at certain planned times, or will they happen randomly (for example, in variable-rate financing, the interest rate is tied to some national figure such as the prime rate)?

Is it possible for you to keep the same interest rate but have graduated payments, perhaps lower in the beginning and rising later on as your income increases?

How Much Can an Adjustable Rate Change?

What are the limits on how much the interest rate on an adjustable-rate loan can increase each year, as well as over the term of the loan? A point and a half or two points should be the maximum increase each year, with a 5% or 6% cap over the term of the loan. Whatever the limits, be sure to negotiate the lowest possible interest rate in the beginning.

Can You Convert to a Fixed-Term Loan Later?

Is it possible for you to convert an adjustable-rate loan to a fixed-rate loan later on if interest rates stabilize? Often, adjustable-rate loans will have this convertibility option.

Can You Extend the Life of a Short-Term Loan?

If you do negotiate a short-term loan, is it possible to extend the term later? In addition, if you negotiate a balloon payment to pay off the principal balance of the loan in 5 or 10 years, can you extend the loan at that same bank for the then-current interest rate without a new title search and other costs?

What Index Is Used to Compute the Adjustable Rate?

In adjustable-rate loans, what index is used to compute the interest rate? You do not want to agree to a volatile index, such as the Consumer Price Index, that may rise and fall continually. It should be a national indicator that moves slowly.

What about Prepayment Penalties?

Is there a prepayment penalty if you pay off your 25- or 30-year loan before the end of the term? You may wish to sell your property 5 or 10 years after the purchase because of a transfer or a job change. Are you going to be penalized one, two, or three points at that time? Often, mortgage lenders will want to have a prepayment clause in the mortgage contract.

What you need to do as a borrower is reduce the points or at least negotiate a time limit of four or five years in which the prepayment penalty would be in effect.

Can Your Loan Be Assumed?

Can the loan be assumed by a qualified purchaser to whom you may wish to sell your property? Most banks have prohibitions in the mortgage contract against such transfers. However, if they are satisfied with the interest rate and have a qualified purchaser, it's an advantage to accept a new signer on the loan. They may require you to remain on the loan. However, the equity position of the loan balance several years down the road makes both your position and the bank's very secure.

Are There Any Unfamiliar Tax Consequences?

Are there any new rules in the tax law, specifically about the deductibility of interest that may adversely affect you? Your local CPA or tax attorney can advise you in this area.

Will You Always Be Able to Afford the Loan?

Finally, consider not only the loan that will get you into the house, but the one you can live with for a long period and whose cost, if variable, is going to rise less than your income rises.

SIX POINTS ON CHOOSING A MORTGAGE

1. Seek a loan with the lowest possible interest cost. Among the many terms and conditions you will negotiate in a mortgage loan, interest is the most important because of its inherent considerable cost over time. The interest amount may be the same on two different types of loans. However, the interest cost over time may be less on a loan ending in 25 years, than one ending in 30 years. Often, the way in which a loan is paid off, such as biweekly payments, can further lessen interest over time.

2. Make sure that the mortgage's total cost for the monthly or biweekly period in which you will pay it (including any points or additional fees that start the loan or mortgage insurance premiums) is one you can afford and will continue to afford though the payments may change in the future.

3. Compare the mortgage to other investment choices. What alternatives are there? Is it worthwhile for you to reduce the down payment, get a larger mortgage, and invest the extra cash you may have? Alternatively, will the rate you invest at be lower than the rate you have to pay for the mortgage, so having less mortgage becomes the wisest investment?

4. Reduce overall interest costs and the principal balance of your mortgage by making as large a down payment as possible. Again, you have to measure a large down payment against alternative investments. Put a minimal amount down to gain more financial strength elsewhere.

5. Be on the lookout for restructuring opportunities. Financing should not be viewed as something that must remain unchanged from the time the property is first bought. There are always opportunities to refinance or restructure your loan with your present lender. You can also pay the loan off with a new loan from another lender at a lower rate. You must always be flexible to take care of any change in the economic environment.

6. Do not burden yourself financially. Your down payment, up-front closing costs, and interest rate must be affordable and in concert with a financial plan that meets your individual needs.

In Chapter 6, we will outline the sources for your mortgage money.

WHERE DO YOU GET YOUR MORTGAGE MONEY? 6

Banks loan most of the mortgages given out in the United States. Many of us think a bank is the only source of financing. However, other options are often less expensive and more flexible. Some sources may take a little creative planning. In this chapter, we will review some of the many different sources of financing and the kinds of mortgages that are offered.

SOURCES FOR YOUR MORTGAGE—FROM BANKERS TO SELLERS

Mortgage money is available from so many different sources that it can make the selection downright confusing. Countless lenders from savings and loans to commercial banks to credit unions stand ready to lend you money.

To find the one that will keep your mortgage costs down, you need to become familiar with some of the choices. Thousands of dollars can be saved over the life of a mortgage just by negotiating a lower interest rate. And, as we saw in Chapter 5, having to pay points for the privilege of being loaned money can hit hard financially.

■ *KEY POINT: The variety of loan sources helps hold down costs.*

As you'll see here, there are a multitude of ways to negotiate low-cost loans.

SOURCES FOR MONEY AND HOW TO APPROACH THEM

There are seven major sources for mortgage loans:

1. Seller financing.
2. Savings banks.
3. Mutual savings banks.
4. Commercial banks.
5. Mortgage brokers.
6. Credit unions.
7. Insurance companies and pension funds.

The following sections describe each of these sources.

Seller Financing

The prime source of financing is the person from whom you buy the property. Often overlooked, the seller is motivated to make a deal and, more times than not, will help you finance. And it's not hard to negotiate. All you have to do is make your offer contingent on the seller's providing a specific amount of financing. It could be the full first mortgage at a fixed rate or assumption of his or her loan with a second mortgage. Both could help with the down payment.

■ *KEY POINT: Sellers often help with financing.*

Often, you can negotiate a better interest rate with a seller than with a bank. If you're dealing with a real estate agent, he or she may discourage you from asking the seller for help. After all, agents are bound by law to work for the seller. Even agents are surprised at how frequently sellers are willing to help.

■ *KEY POINT: You can get a better interest rate from a seller.*

A seller who needs to get out has a motivation to help with financing. An additional benefit is that the seller can defer some of his or her taxable gain over time. For example, if the seller gives a buyer an 8-year mortgage on 90% of the property's value, the seller can spread the profits of the sale over each of those 8 years instead of having to declare a lump-sum profit that would be taxed at a much higher rate.

■ *KEY POINT:*   *When the seller gives the loan, he or she can save taxes.*

Savings Banks

Savings banks, called by different names in each region of the country, make the most residential loans in the United States. Almost all communities have such banks, and mortgage officers are active in selling their money to you. They make home and investment loans.

■ *KEY POINT:*   *Savings banks loan the most mortgage money.*

Savings banks are one of the easiest institutions to approach. Go and discuss your needs with a neighborhood banker before you start looking for property. Ask about the availability of money, current interest rates, and the types of properties the bank gives mortgages for. If you set up a rapport with a mortgage officer before you buy, you will find it much easier and quicker to make the actual commitment once you choose the property.

■ *KEY POINT:*   *Savings banks are prepared to act fast.*

Mutual Savings Banks

A major source of mortgage money is the mutual savings bank. Like savings banks, they may be called by a variety of names, such as, mutuals, savings banks, and cooperative banks in different areas of the country. All have a distinction that separates them from some of their more commercial competitors: They are owned by the depositors. They are not corporations with stockholding owners. They operate as large joint ventures or partnerships similar to cooperatives. They are like the New England town meeting. Depositors have a say in who are the directors of the bank and encourage good public relations for the bank in their community.

■ *KEY POINT:* *Mutual savings banks are like cooperatives, and they will work with you if you deposit funds with them.*

These banks are small, although many have become larger by merging with other banks. Like true savings and loans (S&L), they have easily accessible offices and mortgage officers who are anxious to place their money in the community. As with savings and loans, they're easy to approach. However, they often require you to open a savings account in a nominal amount to be eligible for a loan.

Commercial Banks

Commercial banks, in their desire to expand beyond checking accounts and business and car loans, have steadily moved into the mortgage market. They are more conservative than savings banks, but many borrowers have found them to be excellent sources for money, particularly for larger investments. They also make residential loans. If you need an extra $25,000 or $40,000 to fix up a house, they are the place to go.

■ *KEY POINT:* *Commercial banks aggressively loan for home improvements and, increasingly, mortgages.*

Commercial banks, perhaps because of their history of loaning money to business, are often more likely than savings banks to loan money to finance a two-car garage or mother-in-law apartment.

You approach them as you would the other banks, with information about the property and your financial circumstances.

You can negotiate interest rate and terms, but be aware that they need more profitability than other banks. They're stockholder-owned corporations that seek a return on invested capital. This often makes their interest rate slightly higher than the mutual or cooperatively owned banks. Although they must be competitive, they are one of the more versatile sources of mortgage funds. Perhaps their experience in dealing with business owners for many years has made them flexible in varying the terms and conditions of a loan.

■ *KEY POINT: Commercial banks can be approached for personal loans and second mortgages.*

Mortgage Brokers

Mortgage brokers are a cross between an institution and an individual. They don't usually have large, banklike buildings; more often, they're located in an office storefront. Mortgage brokers originate loans with money they have usually borrowed from a commercial source. They then sell the loans to large institutional investors such as insurance companies.

They act as an agent brokering mortgages. That is, they do all the origination work for a fee. They usually place large loans on investment property, apartments, condominiums, and commercial stores.

■ *KEY POINT: The mortgage broker acts as a go-between with large banks for investment loans.*

They are not always a good source for home loans. They usually prefer large deals, and their rates are not always competitive. They usually charge 1% to 2% beyond the normal cost of money to include their fee.

Mortgage brokers are fond of charging points. After dealing with them, you may feel they want to make it as hard as possible for you to negotiate a loan. However, for certain types of projects that are beyond the scope of your local savings bank, they can be a practical source. They can cut red tape to a minimum, assuring you a quick commitment.

■ *CAUTION NOTE: Mortgage brokers often charge high fees for their service.*

Credit Unions

Credit unions can be your prime source of mortgage money if you are a member or eligible to be one. Credit unions are often established for employees of a large business or university. They're like a miniature bank run for the benefit of their employee members.

Large companies such as General Motors and IBM, most state universities, and even government entities have credit union money. They aren't as experienced in placing mortgages as full-fledged mortgage or savings banks, but this can work to your advantage. Any information you can give them on the value of the property and your own economic resources goes a long way in gaining a favorable decision. Credit unions don't usually do the research themselves.

■ *KEY POINT: If you're a member, a credit union is an excellent source for a modestly priced loan.*

Insurance Companies and Pension Funds

Two other sources of money remain: insurance companies and pension funds. They usually loan money on investment projects that require $500,000 and up. In fact, they're almost the sole source of money for projects of several million or more.

It's possible but rare to get a mortgage commitment from either source in less than several weeks. The necessary paperwork and the formal appraisal work involved in granting such large sums of mortgage money takes time. Careful calculations assure the insurance company or pension fund is secure in the investment. All this documentation is time consuming.

■ *KEY POINT: Insurance companies and pension funds often loan large amounts under complex arrangements.*

Your proposal and the work involved in the insurance company's or pension fund's decision making follow the same process described in Chapter 1 but are larger in scope. A loan officer or investment committee can give overnight approval, but often more investigative time is required. Many people in different levels of management are involved in approving these loans. The step-by-step way in which an insurance company considers a loan is the same as the procedure for getting a mortgage from your local S&L.

When seeking a major decision, a group of investors must provide detailed architectural plans and many financial projections including building and zoning approval from local authorities.

Most insurance companies that place loans of this type have real estate departments or have appointed someone in your region to act for them. Fees are charged for the preliminary investigations by the insurance company or trust fund. Although these fees alone may be thousands of dollars, they make the loan process move forward. Also, they are evidence to the insurance company or fund of the seriousness of your intentions.

■ *CAUTION NOTE: Insurance companies often charge heavy fees up front to negotiate loans with them.*

The insurance company is in the business of lending money; approach it with the help of competent attorneys, architects, and builders.

HOW TO SELECT THE BEST MONEY SOURCE

Not all seven sources for mortgage money may be available in your community. However, you may have one or two savings banks and a commercial bank, perhaps even a credit union where you work. You may be in a small community where there's only one source or in a suburb of a large city that has numerous firms of each description.

An excellent way to select a source for a mortgage is to become familiar with several before you find the property you wish to purchase. This way, you don't limit your choice to a single institution until you've checked the most favorable interest rates or terms, and you set up contact with the different mortgage officers. It is their job to help you; more important, they can often take your side and support your needs, influencing those in the bank who make the final decision.

You must develop a relationship with a banker. It is proper to take him or her to lunch; take the time to make him or her familiar with you and your finances. Loan officers like people who come to them prepared and who think ahead enough to make their job easier—these are most often the people who are never late with payments.

- *CAUTION NOTE: Don't deal with just one institution until you investigate the mortgage plans in all.*
- *KEY POINT: Personal contact with an individual banker is critical for negotiations.*

Sometimes you cannot do this preliminary work. If you are coming in from out of town on a weekend looking for a new house, you'll likely spend most of your time looking at the real estate advertisements. You'll probably be tied up with real estate agents. Still, try to visit a bank or two. If you cannot, get as much information as you can from the agents or even sellers about what's happening in the local mortgage market.

This extra effort prevents you from rushing the decision. Shop for both the right property and rates. Now is the time to assemble the information for comparing loans on the basis of rate, points, and terms.

- *KEY POINT: When viewing property in a new area, visit banks too.*

When you look at a house, find out where the existing loan is placed. Next to the seller, the bank that has the money invested in the property is often the prime source of funds. Since a portion of the money needed for a new mortgage is already placed on the property and the bank often needs to add a little more to get a slightly higher interest rate on the whole amount, loan officers are anxious to do business. In fact, they are often flexible enough to reduce or even cut points.

■ *KEY POINT: The bank that holds the existing financing is the leading possibility for new money.*

GOVERNMENT HELP

The Federal Housing Administration (FHA) provides lending help to many mortgage borrowers. An FHA loan is easy to qualify for. It is limited to $67,500 to $124,875 depending on the particular market area. You can apply 29% of gross, monthly income to mortgage payments and 41% to all debt payments. In conventional financing, those proportions are often limited to 28% and 36%, respectively.

Down payments can vary. You can put down only 3% of the first $25,000 of the loan and 5% of the balance. You can finance up to 57% of closing costs. Assuming closing costs of 4%, you may pay $1,100 at the closing on a typical $85,000 loan. FHA mortgage insurance tacks 3.8% of the loan up front and charges an additional 0.5% for 5 to 10 years, a total of almost $60 a month on an $85,000 loan.

A strategy to consider if you have a low down payment is to get a conventional loan. Private mortgage insurance, required when the down payment is less than 20%, often costs less than FHA insurance, while interest rates are comparable.

The Federal National Mortgage Association (Fannie Mae) has a special program called the "3/2 Option," which allows you to get up to 2 of the 5 percentage points of the down payment from a relative or public agency. The 3/2 Option is available through local lenders if your household income doesn't exceed 115% of the median in your area.

ASSUMING THE EXISTING MORTGAGE

You don't always have to start a fixed-rate loan with a new source. Many existing loans are assumable, meaning you can take them over for the remaining term of the loan.

Most loans granted before the early 1980s were conventional fixed-rate loans. Many of these mortgages can be assumed as long as it isn't specifically prohibited in the agreement. Even later, more recent, loans can be assumed, although the lender's permission may be required.

■ *KEY POINT: Mortgages can be assumed unless the agreement specifically prohibits it.*

Your lawyer should check any loan you might want to assume and determine whether it can be taken over without being called, that is, canceled so the balance must be immediately paid.

■ *CAUTION NOTE: Beware of nonassumption clauses in mortgage agreements.*

Many older loans don't trigger a payoff on transfer. For many years, when interest rates were stable (without dramatic swings in direction from one year to another), banks allowed assumptions, primarily by just overlooking them. They were mildly irritating. After all, why would someone take over an existing loan when he or she could borrow more at the same rate?

Today's rates are usually much higher than those stated in old loans. The balance of an existing loan, however, is likely to be less than the price you will pay for the property. So if you do assume an existing loan, you may want the seller to help you with some additional financing, such as a second mortgage, to make up the difference between the balance of the old loan and the down payment.

■ *KEY POINT: Assumptions of loans have become more common as rates have risen.*

■ *KEY POINT: The seller will often make up the difference when you assume a mortgage.*

Your rate on the assumed mortgage is likely to be favorable. You can easily offer the seller a tempting rate on the second mortgage. When you combine the rates of the two mortgages, you will be paying less than you would in paying for a new mortgage. You could even pay a bit more for the property because this lower interest rate makes your effective cost of the property less.

In some areas, assumable loans have been specifically excluded in mortgage agreements. Therefore, it is difficult to find property with a loan you can take over. It depends on the local situation. However, next to the seller giving total financing (see Chapter 9), assuming an existing loan is one of the first steps you should consider in buying any property.

■ *KEY POINT: Always investigate the possibility of assuming the existing loan.*

Some lenders call loans "assumable" but reserve the right to renegotiate all the terms on transfer. Be sure to check the original loan contract. Many states have enacted legislation to try to end this problem, but it still exists in some areas.

MAKE YOUR OWN DEAL

In any loan, interest rates are a primary consideration. This is especially true for a fixed-rate loan, where the interest rate will remain constant for years. One way you can drive down the rate is to limit the bank's exposure—the ratio of loan to sale price.

You can do this by putting down a larger down payment, such as 30% to 40%, thereby limiting the bank's investment to 60% to 70%. If you could put down 50% so the bank need only invest another 50%, you could get the lowest interest rate possible.

■ *KEY POINT: Negotiate a lower interest rate by limiting the amount of the mortgage.*

Another way for you to limit the bank's exposure, without putting down a large down payment, is to negotiate a second mortgage with the seller. This eats up some of the down payment. For example, if you put down 10% and received another 25% as a second mortgage, that would leave 65% to obtain as a mortgage from the bank. To keep the payments low, the term of the second mortgage could run for as many years as the first.

■ *KEY POINT: Combine a bank mortgage with seller financing for low interest.*

Since the bank views the property as strong security for the loan, mortgages that are low in comparison to the property's value are also the easiest to negotiate. They don't require as much inspection of either your circumstances or the property because the security for the loan is high. And the bank knows it will be profitable. The mortgage officers don't have to justify their investment in the loan as much as they would normally have to do.

■ *KEY POINT: Mortgages with lower exposure for the bank are easier to negotiate.*

Under these circumstances, the paperwork can be completed much more quickly. Often you can gain a commitment the same day you present the request.

In the next few chapters, we'll look at the various kinds of mortgages and where you go to get them. Acquiring knowledge not only about sources but also about the ways lenders construct financing will help negotiate a superior mortgage program.

GETTING CREATIVE WITH CONVENTIONAL FINANCING

When you need financing to buy a home or an income property, institutional lenders stand ready to loan you what you need. Mortgage officers, who are easy to approach and who are skilled at making loans, are prepared (within the parameters of a bank's lending policy) to help you.

THE FIRST CHOICE: DO YOU WANT TO GAMBLE ON INTEREST RATES?

First, do you want the conventional fixed-rate loan? After all, most banks also give adjustable-rate loans. In the ARM, the monthly payments vary according to a changing interest rate dependent on overall economic indexes. By contrast, the fixed-rate loan is based on a constant rate of interest negotiated at the time the loan is made.

■ *KEY POINT:* *Choosing between a fixed-rate mortgage and an ARM is a major decision when dealing with the bank.*

Usually, adjustable loans are reviewed every quarter or six months and, based on some national economic index such as the 1-year Treasury bill rate, may move downward or upward. If the interest rate moves upward in an adjustable-rate mortgage, you may have to face a higher monthly payment, as the bank sets its new interest rate on your loan.

■ *CAUTION NOTE: Over time, the rate in an ARM is likely to move upward.*

If you wish to gamble that interest rates will fall, the adjustable-rate loan, often starting a point or so below average rates, may be your bet. You gamble it may fall further.

If you feel interest rates are going to rise, you may choose a fixed-rate loan. Although it is a point or so higher than the adjustable rate, it will remain at the negotiated interest rate until you sell your property, pay off the loan, or refinance it.

■ *KEY POINT: Fixed-rate loans are preferable when you expect average rates to increase.*

The future of interest rates is not the only factor in the decision. The other advantages of a fixed-rate loan may be more important considerations. You may desire the predictability of a constant payment for your monthly budget.

The stability of the payment can be a benefit. As time goes on, the money you earn makes these payments appear smaller. Since the value of the dollar declines over time—the dollar buys less each year—this, combined with your rising income, helps the fixed payment.

■ *KEY POINT: The stability of the fixed payment may benefit you in the future.*

If you have an adjustable-rate loan, a rising national rate may boost your interest rate. It could be much higher than the percentage you could have negotiated for a fixed-rate loan when you started the loan. Among the potential problems that must concern you, the chance of your mortgage payment rising is one you can avoid.

Now, will rates go down? Perhaps, and we will talk more about this and the advantages of an adjustable-rate loan in the next chapter.

WHEN THE CONVENTIONAL LOAN MAY BE BEST FOR YOU

A clear benefit of the fixed-rate loan is its absolute stability and predictability. You know what your mortgage payments are and don't have to worry about any changes occurring in the future.

As interest rates decline, you can do what many others with a fixed-rate loan do: simply renegotiate to a lower interest rate. This is essentially applying for a new loan. A bank may require an updated title search and new loan agreement. They may also charge points, either to satisfy the prepayment condition in the old loan, or simply to start the "new" loan. Often, however, on refinancing with the same bank, many of these loan fees are waived.

■ *KEY POINT:*   *Fixed-rate mortgages can be refinanced.*

At the time you decide to refinance, you should weigh whether the lower interest rate, and hence lower monthly payment, is worth paying several thousand dollars in points.

■ *CAUTION NOTE:*   *Banks often charge points on refinancing.*

Of the loans started today, the vast majority are fixed rate; less than a third are adjustable rate. We can't predict how this proportion may change. It is based on borrowers' perceptions of where the interest rate may go and the desire for banks to make one type of loan over the other.

If you want to negotiate a monthly payment that will fit into your budget without having to worry whether it's going to increase, then the conventional loan may be the best choice.

SHOPPING FOR THE CONVENTIONAL LOAN

Shopping for the right loan entails two tasks. The first project is to gather all the technical information about the different banks—the programs that are available, how much interest is charged, and what points are charged. The second project is to find the right banker to do business with. Banks are not just huge institutions. Like most enterprises, they are composed of people. When you negotiate a mortgage loan, you usually talk with one individual, who works with you throughout the entire transaction.

■ *KEY POINT: Loan shopping includes getting the right information and making personal contact with a banker.*

Getting a loan is not like going up to a teller and discussing the amount of your checking account. Much more information will pass back and forth. Make lists. They will help you through these negotiations.

If you can choose a bank and banker before you buy, all the better. If you have agreed to purchase the property and then have 10 to 20 days in which to secure financing, you need to be prepared.

Your first list can be the various banks that offer conventional fixed-rate mortgages (they will probably also offer adjustable-rate mortgages). When discussing the best financial arrangements, you should consider both kinds.

■ *KEY POINT: Make a list of the mortgage banks in your area and what they offer.*

All mortgage banks offer conventional fixed-rate loans. They advertise their loans and interest rates in the local newspapers. They're looking for your business. In some areas, newspapers publish a weekly list of current bank charges (interest rates and points) that provides a good starting place for comparisons. However, the best way to get this information is to initiate contact by calling the banks themselves.

You may have six or more banks on your list. Once you have selected the bank to approach, establish rapport with one of its mortgage officers.

To negotiate your way out of an expensive prepayment penalty, whether in selling or refinancing, it's preferable not to do business with a stranger but with someone who will integrate the bank's requirements with your needs.

■ *KEY POINT: The banker you work with should not be a stranger.*

SELECTING YOUR BANKER

To find banks eager to do business with you, look for the display advertisements in your local paper, where you will see many offerings of interest rates and different mortgages. Bankers, as well as real estate agents, are competing for your business. It's their job to sell you money.

How should you choose one? Begin by talking to the mortgage officers of several banks to see with whom you are most comfortable. In choosing a bank, remember that the lowest interest rate is not the only factor. Other terms and conditions—such as points, assumability, and length of term—also affect a mortgage's value and suitability.

You want a banker with whom you have rapport, someone who will listen and be receptive to your requirements. You look for a rapid decision by the bank. You also want a mortgage that has the lowest possible rate, a minimum of points, and no prepayment penalty. To do this, you must establish a minimum measure of trust and confidence with the banker of your choice. You start by getting out and meeting representatives from various banks.

■ *KEY POINT: Besides favorable rates and terms, you want a banker with whom you can negotiate.*

■ *KEY POINT: Establish trust and confidence with the banker.*

Most banks in a given area don't vary much in their interest rates for a fixed-rate loan. Unfortunately, they know what the other banks charge. It may look like price fixing, but it's not. All they do is check the newspaper to find out what their competitors are charging.

A word of caution. A difference of half a point or even a full point shouldn't make you run to the bank with the lower rate. Usually, such differences in rates are made up by charging points.

■ *CAUTION NOTE: Beware of a low interest rate alone—differences are usually made up in points.*

HOW TO NEGOTIATE DOWN PAYMENTS AND INTEREST RATES

When a bank gives a fixed-rate loan, the loan officer often has determined the percentage of a property's value that the bank will loan. For example, most banks readily give an 80% loan. This means that they expect you to provide the other 20% in cash. However, this is not always true, as we will shortly see. Normally, if the bank verifies the value of the property, they will loan you the 80% balance.

■ *KEY POINT: Most banks normally lend 80% mortgages.*

Banks have special programs where they will lend up to 90% and even 95% in some cases. Private and government mortgage insurance programs guarantee to the bank that the loan will be paid off in case of default.

■ *KEY POINT: With private loan guarantees, banks often lend up to 95%.*

In buying your first home or investment property, you may need to get as much money as possible from the bank. In your proposal, you should stress the high value of the property and your strong economic circumstances and ability to pay.

A 90% loan has a quarter or half a point higher interest rate than the 80% loan. Because of the greater amount of money overall, payments are slightly higher. In your proposal, emphasize you can make those higher payments.

■ *CAUTION NOTE: Higher interest rates usually accompany 90% loans.*

Although interest rates are fixed, you often can reduce them by choosing a different loan program. The interest can vary, depending on the amount of mortgage required from the bank. You need to weigh each situation. For example, you might get one loan at 8% but with a 4% prepayment penalty, which would affect sale of the property for the following 10 years. Weigh this plan against a 9% loan with no penalties.

■ *KEY POINT: In some banks, interest rates are negotiated downward by offering points.*

If all other factors are equal and you expect to make a change in real estate four or five years down the road, perhaps due to some job consideration, you'd be better off taking the higher interest rate.

WHAT TO DO WHEN THEY ASK FOR POINTS

To us as consumers, points are a horror. These extra percentage points, charged as a one-time fee, are objectionable and expensive. And, too often, they are requested in granting a fixed-rate loan, but not an ARM. The bank's justification for points is paperwork and overhead costs—but why for one loan and not the other? The answer is that you're going to pay one way or the other.

■ *CAUTION NOTE: Points are usually requested only on fixed-rate loans.*

The idea behind mortgage financing is that banks earn their profit on the interest rate they gain over time. Then why charge points? Simple: It's the latest wrinkle to gain profit above and beyond the interest rate. Maybe if they didn't have so many branch offices, they wouldn't feel so pressured.

■ *CAUTION NOTE:* *Banks charge points to earn greater profits and to pay for burdensome overhead.*

However, the news is not all bad. Points, even more than interest rates, are negotiable and discretionary. They are not mandated by law and have nothing to do with the basic interest rate of the loan. They don't relate to the bank's cost of money as they do to overhead. The one-time bank fee of two or three points is small compared with the interest earned over the life of the loan even though the fee seems huge to the borrower.

■ *KEY POINT:* *Points can be negotiated downward, depending on their purpose.*

When loan shopping, ask exactly what these points are for and what programs are available without these charges. Specifically, the penalty of paying points when you refinance or sell in the future is a provision a bank can agree to dispense with. Many disappointed borrowers have found a few years down the road that it costs them thousands of dollars as a one-time charge to get out of the loan or to refinance it. Keep in mind, however, that if a bank will give you a lower interest rate, it may be worth paying points.

■ *CAUTION NOTE:* *Always try to negotiate prepayment points out of your mortgage agreement.*

How points are charged, how many of them are charged, and what length of time they apply are all issues that you must negotiate early on, before you decide on a loan and sign the mortgage agreement.

THE BENEFITS OF LESS RED TAPE

The way to cut red tape is to detail facts about the property you wish to buy and your economic situation. Certainly, each bank has its own application to fill out, but the information requested is superficial. It doesn't allow you to detail superior qualifications of yourself or the property.

Most borrowers rely on the bank's investigative powers, not only to research the property but to assess their personal financial situation. They assume the bank knows everything. Often, you will be surprised by what they don't know. Your proposal will fill in the gaps. It lessens the need for some of this investigative work, reducing a burden of the bank.

■ *CAUTION NOTE: Banks are not research experts.*

Remember that banks are concerned with three items: (1) the value of the property, (2) your ability to pay the mortgage and what reserves you have, and (3) the profit in it for them. If the bank is assured of the first two and you don't try to get the loan below market rates, the loan officers will feel it is a profitable loan.

■ *KEY POINT: A mortgage proposal cuts red tape and assures the bank of property value, your ability to pay, and the loan's profitability.*

Though red tape depends on each bank's requirements, you can cut as much of it as possible by gaining a mortgage officer's confidence and by providing a detailed proposal about the property and your economic situation.

HOW TO NEGOTIATE THE BEST TERMS

Many people think you can't negotiate a conventional fixed-rate loan. They believe that since banks have been making these loans for years, the rates and terms are set. That isn't true.

The mortgage market today is extremely competitive. Even the larger, more central banks compete with each other in lending smaller banks money at the lowest possible interest rates; these, in turn, are passed on to you. The stiff competition among banks makes it possible for you to negotiate the lowest rate. You may be able to reduce or altogether eliminate the points charged for the origination fee or prepayment penalties. Often, the banks don't feel they can afford to push for this extra money.

■ *KEY POINT: Competition forces banks to negotiate on rates and points.*

The key is to survey all the possible mortgage sources. In this way, you are most likely to find one or more lenders who are willing to give you a mortgage at a better rate and terms.

And keep negotiating. If you have made a preliminary survey of the banks and have become acquainted with mortgage officers before you actually proceed with the property purchase, your deal will go through faster.

■ *KEY POINT: Negotiating with all sources is the best way to get the most advantageous deal.*

Sometimes it helps to let a banker know you're talking to other bankers—gently playing one against the other. This is a delicate maneuver, as you don't want to offend anyone or otherwise jeopardize your relationship with a mortgage officer.

You never want to give bankers the impression that you're a wheeler-dealer. Even if you're buying an investment property, it's still preferable to be modest. When negotiating, make your contacts feel that they have something special to offer and that's why you want to negotiate with them. It's a superb way to get them to see your point of view and to come up with the lower interest rate and fairest terms.

■ *CAUTION NOTE: Don't upset the relationship of trust with a banker.*

WHAT YOUR BANKER CAN AND CANNOT DO

Bankers are in the business of making sound financial decisions. They can loan you a reasonable percentage of a property's selling price within the general parameters that their individual bank or state banking board has established. The percentage of loan to sale price amount is generally a maximum of 90%, although certain loan programs go up to 95%. Some government loans, such as the FHA with a 3% down payment, are even higher.

Banks usually loan between 80% and 90% of the sales price. They cannot loan you 100%. If you only have $5,000 to put down on a $100,000 property, they cannot in most cases loan you the other 95% unless the property has been valued at more than $100,000.

■ *CAUTION NOTE: Banks can never loan you the full value of the property.*

You are also limited in how much you can negotiate on interest. Bankers cannot go below what they pay for the money. And when they relend it to you, they must add 2% to 4% to cover overhead and profit. For example, if a bank uses its own funds and pays its depositors an average of 4% to 5%, it is likely to charge another 3% to 4% for overhead, resulting in a rate of 7% to 8%. However, if the bank must borrow the money from another bank at, for example, 6% to 7%, then the rate it charges will be 10% to 11%.

■ *CAUTION NOTE: Banks have a lower limit on their interest rates.*

Negotiation for the optimal terms can only occur within certain limits. The bank is most likely to be flexible on the issue of points. The bank may reduce or drop those charged for the origination of the loan or forgive them should the property be refinanced or sold at a later time. Too many borrowers wait until later to negotiate these prepayment points. They should be handled at the loan's origination.

■ *KEY POINT:* *Banks can be more flexible on points than on interest rate.*

Banks also have the discretionary power to allow you to assume a supposedly nonassumable loan. Many states are beginning to enact laws permitting the direct assumption of loans. Banks, in feeling this pressure, are in some cases allowing assumptions that they might not otherwise have agreed to. It is a matter of negotiation.

INSIDE TIPS ON CONVENTIONAL LOANS

The guidelines for getting a conventional loan involve common sense. First, see if you can take over an existing mortgage either by assuming it or taking it "subject to," that is, by taking over payments without assuming liability. You should always explore taking over an old loan. If the loan balance is large enough and the interest rate is low, it can be well worth doing so, even if you have to put down a larger down payment and work out a second mortgage with the seller.

■ *KEY POINT:* *Always first see if you can assume a mortgage.*

If the mortgage you wish to take over has a "due on sale clause," it means that the bank (should you take over the property and change the title) could demand full payment of the balance. The way to avoid this possibility is to negotiate with the bank beforehand. They may very well say no but then surprise you by allowing the transfer with reasonable changes, such as an increase in the interest rate—not to the full current rate but to a rate in between. Also, with an assumed loan, a short term may remain; for example, you may want to extend a 15-year balance to 25 years to make the monthly payments lower.

A smart borrower has the preliminary negotiations out of the way before committing to buy a particular property. Always done by professional investors, this approach also benefits those making an occasional purchase of a house or investment property. The key to getting a favorable interest rate and terms lies in the personal contact you have with a mortgage officer. This can be even more important than the actual choice of bank with which you do business.

■ *KEY POINT: Negotiate with a mortgage officer before you buy.*

The proposal you make up—information on the property, your own financial status, and ability to pay, and a cover letter that recognizes the lender's need to profit from the arrangement—combined with a working relationship with a mortgage officer, goes a long way in getting a favorable and rapid commitment.

■ *KEY POINT: A mortgage proposal is the best way to get a favorable and quick commitment from the bank.*

Occasionally, you will come across a property—usually a new one in a housing development—that a particular bank (with the builder) is offering at a "special" low interest rate, perhaps four or five points lower than normal. Be wary of such loans. Interest rates are based on a profitable economic rationale, and the bank will get its return in other ways. For example, if a 3% rate is offered when average conventional rates are hovering around 8%, the difference may be made up in the sales price. The arrangement works for the bank because the builder kicks back a big fee for each loan processed at the lower rate. Illegal? Not at all, if the deal is divulged to you (even if only at closing); then, however, it's getting late to complain. Is this lower rate a disadvantage to you? Not if you like paying more for a property.

■ *CAUTION NOTE: Unusually low interest rates may mean the fee to the bank is hidden in the selling price.*

In a variation of this arrangement, the bank makes the below-market interest rate good only for a year or two, after which the interest rates go back to their current level. Again, to get this loan, either you or the builder will pay a big fee up front. This, too, might be all right . . . if you want a big shock several years down the road.

■ *CAUTION NOTE: Initially low rates may mean higher ones for the long term.*

In Chapter 8, we will learn about the advantages of adjustable-rate mortgages and how to negotiate them with your bank.

WHAT YOU NEED TO 8
KNOW ABOUT
ADJUSTABLE-RATE
LOANS

Chapter 3 introduced "adjustable" mortgages, officially called adjustable-rate mortgages (ARM) or variable-rate loans (VRL). They are the newest and most complicated forms of mortgages. In all adjustable mortgages, the interest rate is allowed to vary according to a leading interest rate index, often based on a prime or Treasury bill rate. Lenders raise and lower the interest rate on the mortgage based on similar increases and decreases in the index. These mortgage plans usually contain limits, called rate caps, on how far the interest rate can change.

■ *KEY POINT: In an ARM, the interest rate varies according to a national or regional index.*

ARMs have rate caps on two levels: maximum per period (with definition of the period as six months or one year), and life caps (the maximum the lender can raise rates for the entire life of the contract). Too often, a "teaser" or initial low rate is revised upward soon after the mortgage is signed.

■ *CAUTION NOTE: An initial low rate on an ARM often escalates quickly.*

Depending on the lender's particular adjustable mortgage program, the change in the interest rate may result in a change

121

in the monthly payment, the loan term, or the balance of the principal. There are many ways to vary these loans, but they are all tied to a national economic index. As this index number changes, your rate, hence payment, changes. For example, if you negotiate an adjustable-rate loan with a beginning interest rate of 6% and the interest rate of the particular index to which your loan is tied increases, you might suddenly find yourself making payments based on an 8% interest rate. Some banks offer plans in which the interest rate can change every three or six months but the payment only changes every two years. In this case, the monthly payments may not be enough to cover all the interest due, thereby causing the unpaid interest to be added to the loan balance. This negative amortization can often occur when monthly payments are not adjusted at the same time as the interest rate.

■ *CAUTION NOTE:* *Payments that do not keep up with the interest rate in an ARM can cause unpaid interest to be added to the loan balance.*

Always find out the actual annual percentage rate (APR) for your loan. For example, you borrow $90,000 on an adjustable-rate, 25-year mortgage at 6.5% with maximum caps on the interest rate of 2% for every two-year adjustment period and 6% over the term of the loan. Also, you must pay a 2.5% loan fee. Your overall APR for this loan is 10.4%, far above the initial 6.5%.

THE DIFFERENT ADJUSTABLE-RATE LOANS

Adjustable-Rate Mortgage (ARM)

In a typical adjustable-rate mortgage, an initial interest rate is negotiated at the beginning of the loan, then adjusted according to the particular index at fixed intervals during the life of the loan. This index may be an accepted indicator of interest rates, such as the current 90-day Treasury bill rate—the interest the U.S. Treasury pays on its short-term borrowing. In this way, your monthly payment periodically changes based on fluctuations in the overall monetary indicators.

■ *KEY POINT: A common ARM index is the 90-day Treasury bill rate.*

Although the initial rate you pay on an ARM may be lower than on a fixed-rate loan, much of the risk in whether rates will rise or fall is assumed by you. The lender needs less protection against a possible rise in rates. Therefore, banks, to encourage you to choose this loan, lend this money out at a slightly lower rate to start.

■ *CAUTION NOTE: In an ARM, the interest rate may be lower to start, but you assume the risk of a possible rise in rates.*

Graduated Payment Mortgage (GPM)

Another adjustable loan is the graduated payment mortgage. This loan provides for smaller payments at the beginning, which rise in fixed amounts over a set number of years—often 10 years.

■ *KEY POINT: In the graduated payment plan, payments rather than interest rates vary.*

In one GPM plan, the payments increase at 6.5% each year for the first six years of the loan. Eventually, the monthly payments will rise above those of a comparable fixed-rate mortgage.

The lower payment in the beginning is excellent for a young professional starting in an entry-level job—anyone whose salary may be low now but who expects dramatic increases in a few years.

■ *KEY POINT: A GPM allows you to get a mortgage with minimal beginning payments.*

You may wonder when you start paying off the principal. True, in the first few years when the payment is lower, you may not reduce the principal. You may even gain negative amortization and pile up more debt. For example, if your original interest rate is 6.75% but your initial monthly payments are less than they would normally be at the 6.75% rate, the difference eats up any principal that would have been paid. This gives you a small deficit that is added to the loan balance. For example, if you started with a $55,000 loan with the lower payment schedule, you might actually owe $56,000 at the end of the first year.

■ *CAUTION NOTE: Negative amortization, the adding on of unpaid interest, can occur in graduated payment plans.*

This small deficit does not mean this loan program is bad. You have had the advantage of smaller payments; you can invest that money elsewhere in the meantime. It's money you're not paying to the bank when your salary is low. Later, when you can afford it, you can make full payments. The money itself is usually added at the end of the loan and you may not plan to keep the property that long.

The disadvantage of this loan is the gamble that your salary will rise. In a few years, your payments will increase to the normal payment, based on the interest rate you negotiated at the beginning. At that time, the loan will appear more like a fixed-rate, conventional loan. You must then have the income to support these higher payments.

■ *CAUTION NOTE: In a GPM, you gamble that your salary will increase to meet the larger payments expected later.*

Graduated Payment, Adjustable-Rate Mortgage

This mortgage combines the fixed increase of payments of the GPM with an adjustable interest rate. As in the GPM, unpaid interest from the early years is added to the loan balance.

In some graduated payment, adjustable-rate mortgages, payments rise a fixed amount each year for several years; others set lower payments in the beginning years. In this mortgage, as with many adjustable loans, there are many variations.

■ *KEY POINT: Like the GPM, the graduated payment, adjustable-rate mortgage sets payment increases and adds unpaid interest to the loan balance.*

Pledged-Account Mortgage (PAM)

The pledged-account mortgage is a special kind of graduated payment loan. It is a way in which the unpaid interest, instead of being added onto the loan balance, is automatically withdrawn from a savings account pledged by the borrower. A portion of the borrower's down payment is used to create the savings account.

■ *KEY POINT: Pledged-account mortgages call for a savings account to be pledged for the unpaid interest.*

Elastic Mortgage

A loan similar to the adjustable-rate loan is the flexible or elastic mortgage. In this mortgage, the payments are fixed at a set amount as is a fixed-rate loan. However, the interest rate on which these payments are originally based changes according to a chosen government index. Fixed payments but varying rates change the number of payments you make over the life of the mortgage. As the interest rate declines, you need fewer payments to pay off the same balance. For example, an elastic mortgage with a term of 20 years originally set at 9% will be paid off more quickly, perhaps in 18 years, if the rate drops to 7%.

■ *KEY POINT: In an elastic mortgage, payments remain the same but the payment term varies.*

In an elastic mortgage, you make principal payments more quickly as interest rates drop. As rates increase, you pay off less principal, thereby taking more time for your fixed payments to pay off the loan.

■ *CAUTION NOTE: A rising index causes less principal to be paid, thereby adding payments to the loan.*

This plan combines some of the advantages of both the adjustable-rate and the conventional fixed-rate loans. The payments stay the same, but you can gamble on interest rates varying in the marketplace. The loan is popular with lenders because, as in an ARM, it unburdens them of the risk of changing rates. It also begins with a slightly lower interest rate.

Growing Equity Mortgage (GEM)

Another adjustable loan is called the growing equity mortgage. In a GEM, the equity in your house increases at a faster rate than it normally would under either a constant-payment or flexible-rate loan. You actually pay a little bit more each year than you normally would under either a constant-payment or flexible-rate loan, thus reducing the principal.

This increased amount is based on a predetermined percentage. For example, 6% each year means your loan gets paid off in less time than the originally scheduled term of the loan. The 25-year term might therefore be reduced to 14 or 15 years.

■ *KEY POINT: The higher payments of a growing equity mortgage reduce the principal faster.*

Shared-Appreciation Mortgage (SAM)

In a shared-appreciation mortgage, a lender, in exchange for a lower rate of interest, shares in the property's increase in value. A variation of this is for the lender to share in the equity of the property.

■ *KEY POINT: In a shared-appreciation mortgage, the lender shares in the property's increase in the value in return for giving a low interest rate.*

In return for sharing in the property's appreciation, the lender gives the borrower a lower rate of interest than that on a conventional fixed-rate mortgage. SAMs usually require that a portion of the interest due be contingent on property appreciation. When the property is sold, refinanced, or has matured, the borrower must pay the lender the agreed-on share of the appreciation. Payments on SAMs are long term but may balloon in 5 to 10 years, depending on what is negotiated when the loan is set up.

■ *CAUTION NOTE: Depending on the agreement, a SAM may allow the loan balance to balloon before the end of the term.*

With most banks, you can negotiate what the interest rate will be, the term of the mortgage, and how much appreciation they will receive. Since future appreciation is unknown, the difference between the initial interest rate and the effective, or real, rate is difficult to predict. Initially low payments may increase dramatically if the lender's share of appreciation and loan balance are refinanced at a conventional rate.

■ *KEY POINT: Most banks offering SAMs allow you to negotiate interest rate, terms, and amount of appreciation due.*

In choosing a shared-appreciation mortgage, you must weigh the value of the lower interest rate against the potential appreciation you will give up. If average fixed rates are 9% and you're only offered a 7.5% loan, it's no benefit to you if you have to give up one-quarter of any appreciation. This is particularly true if neighboring property has been rising 3% to 5% per year. The 1.5% interest is a small price to pay to gain the increase in value.

There are other variations of the adjustable-rate or adjustable-payment loan. If you feel any of these are of benefit to you, discuss them fully with your banker. Be aware, however, that the adjustable-rate loan often favors the bank. That's why mortgage officers push it so hard and discount points so easily. They want you to take on the risk of whether rates rise or fall.

■ *CAUTION NOTE: Many adjustable-rate or adjustable-payment mortgages favor the lender.*

When interest rates are high and you feel they will come down, then consider one of these loans. However, if rates are down and inevitably will rise, the risk may not be worth it. Let's see what precautions you can take to protect yourself in assuming the risk of an ARM.

WHY ARMs HAVE SUBSTANTIALLY LOWER RATES

The initial interest rate on an adjustable- or variable-rate mortgage, like a fixed-rate loan, is based on the lender's cost of funds. Specifically, it is based on what the bank must pay to its depositors or another bank.

Historically, mortgage interest rates have not risen much, except in the past 20 years. The modern, robust economy has put the banks under inflationary pressure. They need to protect themselves against the rising tide of higher interest rates. Therefore, they have invented "adjustable" loans tied to national indexes.

■ *CAUTION NOTE: Adjustable loans are predicated on the theory that rates will continue to rise.*

To induce you to opt for the adjustable-rate loan, the banks offer a lower interest rate in the beginning. For up to a year, it may charge two or three points below the rate set for a fixed-rate mortgage. Sometimes, it is four or five points below the fixed rate. However, after an initial grace period, any of these lower rates can change dramatically, by 1.5% to 2% a year. As you saw in Chapter 4, the cut-rate bonuses of four or five points sometimes disappear within a year. To protect yourself, study and discuss carefully with your banker and lawyer the fine print of any of these adjustable-rate mortgages to see exactly how they are structured.

■ *CAUTION NOTE: After the first several years, rates on adjustable loans can rise significantly.*

Lenders, such as thrifts or savings and loans, who prefer to hold mortgages in their own portfolios, suffer in fixed-rate markets. Because ARMs present less risk, many thrifts push, if not oblige, their borrowers to accept adjustable-rate loans, no matter what may be preferable. You may need to insist they make you a fixed-rate loan or lose you as a customer. Although they then may shed the interest rate risk by selling your loan in the secondary market, they will continue to service the loan by collecting payments.

Mortgage bankers seldom keep loans in their portfolios, but instead sell them in the secondary market. They hold onto the servicing rights and thereby generate an income stream over the life of the loan. Mortgage bankers make a higher profit than thrifts because they deal in larger volumes.

■ *CAUTION NOTE: Some lenders offer low initial rates on adjustable loans because they want you to borrow this way.*

LESS RISK THAN YOU THINK

Much of what's been said so far about adjustable-rate mortgages has been derogatory. They have their place, but the problem with them is that their early, low rates are often simply inducements that soon vanish.

These programs are popular; they're heavily promoted by the banks because an adjustable loan protects the bank against interest rates rising. And rates have traditionally risen; throughout this century, rates have slowly increased. In recent years, however, they have gone down. Many borrowers have benefited from this fluctuation. In principle, to profit from an ARM, you have to hit it when rates are high and hope for a low soon.

■ *CAUTION NOTE: Adjustable-rate loans protect banks from rising interest rates.*

The news, then, is not all bad. A few years ago, rates reached peaks of 15% and 16%. They are lower now, since inflation has eased. They may continue to slide for the short term. If this continues, you may benefit. For example, if you start a loan at 10%, it's conceivable the index that determined this rate will slowly decrease. Your current rate might then come down to 6.5%, thereby lowering your payments and reducing the amount of principal on your loan.

■ *KEY POINT:* *You can benefit in the short term if you get an ARM when rates are high but about to decrease.*

RATES ARE TIED TO THE FINANCIAL MARKET

Lenders vary in the index they use to determine your rate, albeit indirectly. A common index is the 90-day Treasury bill rate—what the U.S. Treasury pays on its short-term borrowing. Other indicators are based on 6-month and 1-year Treasury bills. Another is the home loan bank board's national average contract percentage. A more stable and less variable rate than some of these is the rate on a 3-year U.S. Treasury security. In some way, each indicator is tied to an overall national market for money. As each varies, the particular rate of your ARM is adjusted at fixed intervals.

■ *KEY POINT:* *Adjustable mortgages can be tied to one of various national indicators.*

In some ARM agreements, lenders have the right to change the index during a loan. A lender would only do this to gain a higher interest rate for the bank. Check your mortgage agreement closely to see that only one index will be used for the life of the loan. You don't want the rules changed midway through the game.

■ *CAUTION NOTE:* *Some ARM agreements allow the lender to change indexes during the loan.*

When you face an adjustment, you can often approximate what your new rate should be. For example, if your loan is indexed to the 1-year Treasury issue now at 3.75% and your lender's margin is 2.5 points (overhead and profit), the rate on your loan is 6.25%.

RATE FLUCTUATION

At the onset of a loan, it's almost pointless to attempt to predict which way interest rates will go. People often choose an adjustable-rate mortgage because they feel rates will go down. However, you must be prepared for either alternative.

■ *CAUTION NOTE: Rates in the national marketplace can vary significantly.*

As a rough rule, rising inflation causes higher rates, while falling inflation lowers rates. It's hard to come to any fixed rule; short-term fluctuations in the national economy are among the many factors that influence mortgage interest.

■ *KEY POINT: Inflation is the biggest factor affecting interest rates.*

The basis for interest that you negotiate on your mortgage will be with you for a long time. During 30 years, for example, several rises and falls will occur in the mortgage market. Nevertheless, rates historically have risen and this trend is likely to continue.

■ *CAUTION NOTE: Over the long term, rates are likely to rise.*

HOW TO PROTECT YOURSELF AGAINST RISING RATES

In an ARM, you must protect yourself as much as possible against rising rates. To do this, you negotiate a provision within the mortgage agreement that controls any skyrocketing of your interest rate. This limits the amount of each adjustment that can be made to your interest rate. For example, your ARM might call for the interest rate to be reviewed quarterly or every six months. A limit on the amount your interest rate can change might be $1/2$ of 1%.

■ *KEY POINT: Negotiate a limit on how much the interest rate can rise during any one period.*

A harsh change would be a movement of 2% or 3%. In most cases, you'd like to reduce the limit during an adjustment period, and increase the limit during a period of falling interest rates. Choosing the limit should be based on how you expect rates to behave.

The second limit you want is an overall amount that your interest rate or monthly payment can be raised over the life of the loan. A limit, or cap, of three points over a 25-year period would be favorable. In contrast, with an upward limit of 8 or 10 points, or in a mortgage with no cap at all, your loan could get expensive.

■ *KEY POINT: Negotiate an overall limit on the rise of the interest rate during the term of the mortgage.*

This limit is normally on the interest rate, but it can also be on the dollar amount you pay each month. Protect yourself against the unlimited rise of interest rates or payments by having these provisions in your adjustable-rate mortgage.

ADVANTAGES AND DISADVANTAGES OF ARMs

The biggest disadvantage of an adjustable-rate mortgage is having your interest rate tied to an economic index over which you have no control. Traditionally, rates have risen. If your income is low now but will be higher in the future, then it might be reasonable to take advantage of an ARM.

■ *CAUTION NOTE: In an adjustable mortgage, you have no control over the interest rate.*

In an ARM, you may be constantly worried about changes in the index that affect your rate and the current mortgage market. Bankers promote ARMs because they take the gamble out of lending money. Further, an ARM places the risks of higher payments on the borrower's shoulders.

■ *CAUTION NOTE: In an ARM, you assume the risk of higher rates.*

This type of loan has two advantages. First, if you are willing to gamble on future interest rates, you may benefit if the rates decrease. If you are thinking of selling your home within a few years, then the risk of rising rates may not be so important.

■ *KEY POINT: If rates go down, you benefit by having an adjustable loan.*

The second advantage is that the initial interest rate is lower than that charged for a fixed-rate loan. Depending on the amount of this difference (usually 1.5 to 2.5 points), this can be a real plus in getting started. This is particularly true if the lower rate doesn't automatically end in a set time, such as in a year, and revert to a normal rate.

■ *KEY POINT: You benefit from a lower initial rate in an adjustable loan.*

The following sections discuss some ways in which you can negotiate with lenders to make the ARM more beneficial to you. We'll see how to tailor an adjustable-rate loan that will save you money.

CONVERTING TO A FIXED RATE: THE RENEGOTIABLE MORTGAGE

A recent wrinkle in variable-rate plans is called the renegotiable mortgage. Popular several years ago, this variation of the adjustable-rate mortgage benefits borrowers. Unfortunately, it was too good. Now, it is not widely available but is still offered at some banks.

A renegotiable mortgage has a more conservative schedule than most adjustable mortgages. The amount the interest can change is limited. For example, the rate might swing no more than 1.5% to 2% every two years and no more than 5% to 6% over the entire life of the mortgage. Reducing the allowable change protects you against unreasonable swings.

■ *KEY POINT: Renegotiable mortgages limit the swings in interest rates.*

A rate that changes at less frequent intervals than the adjustable-rate mortgage—only adjusting every two to five years—can be an advantage when interest rates are rising.

A variation of the renegotiable-rate mortgage allows you to negotiate the rate itself at specific intervals. For example, every three years you might have the option of converting your interest rate to the prevailing fixed rate of interest. Your current rate might have risen to 11% and fixed-rate loans might be at 9%, thereby making it beneficial for you to change your rate.

■ *KEY POINT: Some renegotiable mortgages allow the interest rate to be negotiated at certain intervals.*

■ *KEY POINT: Renegotiable mortgages allow the option of converting to a fixed rate.*

Most renegotiable-rate mortgages lock in the rate for several years. In this way, they are more conservative than the full adjustable-rate mortgages. They combine the benefits of an adjustable- and a fixed-rate loan. With them, you can take advantage of a downward slide in interest rates and also have some security against rising interest rates.

■ *KEY POINT: Renegotiable mortgages combine the best of adjustable- and fixed-rate loans.*

The renegotiable-rate mortgage with an optional conversion to fixed rate may be the loan program for you if you think that the burden of varying payments eventually may prove too much of a struggle.

THE ADJUSTABLE BALLOON MORTGAGE

Another variation of the adjustable mortgage is the balloon mortgage. It is similar to a fixed-rate loan in that it starts with a set interest rate and a term of 25 or 30 years. However, at the end of a specific period, perhaps five years, the mortgage "balloons." This means the loan must be paid off. Or, as is commonly done, the amount is refinanced at the current interest rate—in this way, it is an adjustable loan.

■ *KEY POINT: Balloon mortgages call for a new interest rate to be negotiated when the loan balloons.*

In only a few years, not much principal will have been paid. In fact, you will owe an amount close to the original loan that must now be paid to the lender. Banks like to use this technique. This is particularly true if they are nervous about what's happening to the cost of money and their ability to get it. In this case, you may have no choice. Sometimes, it is the only type of loan you can negotiate.

What happens when the money is due? In most balloon mortgages, particularly with banks, the entire loan—interest rate, terms, everything—is renegotiated. It does, however, put you at the mercy of the current rate being charged at the time of renegotiation.

From a bank's point of view, a balloon mortgage is more flexible than a renegotiable mortgage. Here, there aren't any limits on what the interest will be. As a borrower of a balloon mortgage, you gamble that rates won't skyrocket. Without a strict provision in the mortgage agreement, the bank can demand some or all of the money. This forces you to come up with cash or go to another bank to borrow the difference.

■ *CAUTION NOTE: Make sure the mortgage agreement allows the loan to be refinanced at the balloon time.*

Normally, you can refinance the balance, and again, these terms should be spelled out specifically in the mortgage agreement. Sometimes, you can negotiate a lower interest rate because of the low ratio of the amount you borrow compared with the higher value of the property. If the value of the property has risen when you renegotiate and you only need to borrow 50% or 60%, you give the bank excellent security. So, you enhance your chance not only for the continuation of the loan but also for a lower rate.

■ *KEY POINT: An advantage at renegotiation time is that the property's value will likely have risen.*

As in the renegotiable loan, you want a guarantee that you can refinance. And, if possible, commit a limit on how much the interest rate can change.

NEGOTIATING MANAGEABLE PAYMENTS

The reason for having an adjustable-rate loan is to beat the current long-term rate. However, adjustable loans were created by banks to do just the opposite. The banks intend to use these instruments to protect themselves; be aware that they want you to assume the risk.

At some banks, unfortunately, these are the only loans available at a reasonable price, the fixed-rate loan having been made prohibitively expensive. These banks charge much more for interest in a fixed-rate loan than they do in an ARM. They also pile up points on the fixed-rate loan. You are not offered much of a choice—they want you to take the ARM. It's therefore essential for you to know the ins and outs of negotiating an adjustable loan. The information here will prepare you.

■ *CAUTION NOTE: By charging more interest for fixed-rate loans, banks force you to choose an adjustable mortgage.*

If an ARM's adjustment period (when the interest rate is reviewed) is every quarter or six months, ask to have that period extended to a year. Then you can plan more, perhaps refinancing, renegotiating a longer term, or switching to a conventional loan if the rate swings the wrong way. In any event, the full year gives you a longer period in which to plan.

■ *KEY POINT: Longer adjustment periods can benefit the borrower.*

In any ARM, the rate often moves down more slowly than it moves up. As an excess of oil may take some time to drive the price of petroleum down in world markets, it may take a good while before the bank passes on the benefits of lower rates to you. If the cost of oil rises, however, it usually doesn't take too long before higher prices appear at the gasoline pump. The same double standard is at work with interest rates. Banks are rarely enthusiastic about lowering rates. Most are profit-making organizations that will jump at the chance to increase their rates but look for reasons to avoid reducing them. Since you know the index that determines your rate, with resolve you can make sure your rate is dropped as rapidly as it is increased.

■ *CAUTION NOTE: Banks raise interest rates faster than they lower them.*

HOW TO PROTECT YOURSELF AGAINST THE PITFALLS OF ARMs

One of the major pitfalls of an adjustable-rate mortgage is that the interest rate is intricately tied to a particular index. Whatever this index is, it affects your monthly payment. Your protection is to assure, through negotiation, that your rate is limited to reasonable jumps for periods that are as long as possible. For example, a reasonable limit might be no more than 1.5% over five years, with a total increase limit of 5% or 6% over the life of the loan. In this way, you are assured that the increase isn't open-ended.

■ *KEY POINT: Limit interest rate movements to reasonable swings.*

In 10 years, you don't want to end up paying twice as much because your interest rate is adjustable. You protect yourself by negotiating reasonable limits.

In some variable-rate plans, such as the graduated payment mortgage, negative amortization can occur. You might not be paying enough to meet your interest debt and therefore the difference will be added on to the balance of the loan. In the beginning, your payments are set artificially low. Although this may look like a bonus for the first few years, the interest you're not paying is added to your loan balance. Eventually you can pay more than your starting loan balance. However, if your income will rise to meet the later payments, negative amortization can be turned into an advantage.

■ *KEY POINT: Negative amortization can be a plus or a minus, depending on how much income you will make in the future.*

Another advantage of ARMs is that banks lessen origination points or prepayment penalties. Since you're shouldering the risk, they don't want to add more burden. They want you to opt for the adjustable plan so badly they try to make it financially attractive.

■ *KEY POINT: Few or no origination points or prepayment penalties are paid with an adjustable mortgage.*

If prepayment points are included, fight to drop them. At the very least, try to negotiate a guarantee that they will not be charged later, such as on refinancing or sale of the property.

It's possible you might want a new buyer to assume your loan in the future. Transferring an ARM is easier to negotiate with the bank, since the rate is already tied to the chosen index. Try to have this provision spelled out in the mortgage agreement.

■ *KEY POINT: Having no prepayment penalty makes it easier to negotiate for a new buyer to take over your loan in the future.*

Banks are willing to do almost anything to get you to borrow their money on an adjustable basis. Because they don't usually require the points charged in their conventional fixed-rate loan, the ARM may look too good to be true. If anything, this tips you off that the banks will somehow benefit—there's a cost to everything. And in an ARM, it's the hidden cost you must protect yourself against.

■ *CAUTION NOTE: In an adjustable mortgage, you must protect yourself against the hidden cost of a rising interest rate.*

In Chapter 9, we will explore creative financing by sellers.

① — No more than 1.5% INC
over 5 yrs

② = Total inc Limit of
5%   6 - 11 ?
                             ? - 12 !

③ — No prepayment Pts

WHEN THE SELLER 9
GIVES YOU THE
MORTGAGE

The most readily available mortgage money is already in the property. The seller owns this equity. Your mortgage may be there for the asking.

HELP FROM THE SELLER:
A TWO-WAY ADVANTAGE

The seller is in an excellent position to loan you money and should always be asked to do so.

Often, real estate agents say sellers aren't interested in giving mortgages. This frequently just isn't true. When money is tight, interest rates are high, and the banks are making few loans, if any at all, sellers must help out with the financing. To make a sale, they must often give either a full first mortgage or help with secondary financing, whether it involves a residential home, an investment property, a vacation home, or even a lot. Many are ready to make mortgage deals.

■ *KEY POINT: More often than not, sellers are willing to give some form of financing.*

What are some of the many ways sellers can help you finance? The most popular is the second mortgage, where you borrow the difference between what a bank lends and how much you invest as a down payment. For example, the second mortgage may only be 10% to 15% of the purchase price, for a short term of 5 to 10 years, and set at an interest rate near the rate for the first mortgage.

■ *KEY POINT: Second mortgages are the most common form of seller financing.*

Another common variation of the second mortgage bases the monthly payment on a long-term payoff, more than 20 or 30 years. However, the balance comes due in a shorter time, perhaps in three to five years. This ballooning usually works because the amount of the second mortgage is small compared with the first mortgage. You can come up with this balloon payment either by refinancing with the bank that holds the first mortgage or borrowing on a short-term basis from a commercial bank. Either way, equity has built up in your property, more than enough to secure any increase in mortgage funds.

■ *KEY POINT: Second mortgages are often accompanied by balloon-payment provisions.*

■ *CAUTION NOTE: Prepare ahead of time to meet the balloon payment.*

Buyers and sellers can work out financing in many ways. One popular arrangement is for the seller to take back a fixed-rate first mortgage, also called a purchase money mortgage. This works well when the seller doesn't have any more than a small mortgage on the property. He or she can change this equity into a mortgage. This often happens in business property, such as in a small apartment building where the owner is ready to retire and willing to continue a steady return on investment. He or she can do this by giving you the mortgage. The seller changes the investment he has from a physical asset to one on paper—a mortgage guaranteeing a steady income at a good interest rate.

Not all sellers can give the first mortgage. It works when the seller's own mortgage is fully paid off or when any small remaining balance can be covered by a down payment. This chapter offers many alternatives to the seller's offering the complete first mortgage.

■ *KEY POINT:*   *Seller financing benefits both buyer and seller.*

■ *CAUTION NOTE:*   *Little (or no) remaining balance on the existing loan is normally a prerequisite for the seller to give a first mortgage.*

You can also take over a seller's existing financing. You assume or take the mortgage "subject to." Before you approach the bank on any specific takeover, go over every detail of the present mortgage agreement with the seller.

■ *KEY POINT:*   *You often get a low interest rate by assuming a seller's existing mortgage.*

Normally, any proposed purchase is conditional on your getting conventional financing from a bank or the seller. A seller who is anxious to make the sale is more likely to allow you to assume the loan or to give you some amount of the sale price as a second mortgage, sometimes even giving you a full first mortgage. Whether you buy direct or use a real estate agent, always try the seller first.

■ *KEY POINT:*   *Always ask the seller about financing.*

ASSUMING THE SELLER'S MORTGAGE

As shown in Chapter 4, you as a buyer can take the seller's place. You can assume or take "subject to" the financing the seller negotiated at the time he or she originally bought the property. Your main reason to take over is to get a lower interest rate and more favorable terms than those you could soon negotiate.

■ *KEY POINT:*   *Assume the seller's loan when you can.*

Assuming a loan means you accept all legal obligations from the seller. Taking the existing loan "subject to" means the seller's name remains on the loan and you're simply making payments for him. You thereby accept less legal liability yourself.

■ *KEY POINT: Officially, "assuming" means accepting legal responsibility; "subject to" means sharing liability.*

Does transferring a loan hurt the seller? Not at all. The seller can get the property sold and you as a buyer get both the loan and a favorable interest rate.

In assuming a loan, you often must put up more cash than you would if you took out a new mortgage. You have to weigh a larger down payment and the lower payments of the existing loan against a smaller down payment but higher payments for a bigger loan and higher interest rate on a new loan. For example, if you take out a new, 20-year, fixed-rate mortgage for $60,000 at 11%, your monthly payments would be $399, instead of $347 for the same balance on an older 7.5% loan. Furthermore, by assuming an existing loan, you will pay off the balance faster and thus will build equity more quickly. Granted, you can often borrow more than the old balance on a new loan. However, there will be a big difference in payments because of the higher interest rate.

■ *CAUTION NOTE: Assuming an existing loan may mean a larger down payment.*

■ *KEY POINT: The advantages include lower monthly payments, faster equity buildup, and less time until maturity.*

To take advantage of the lower rate but not have such a large down payment, negotiate a second mortgage in addition to the takeover. You can do this with the seller or the bank.

■ *KEY POINT: A second mortgage can make up the difference between the loan you assume and a reasonable down payment.*

In any second mortgage, you may likely pay higher interest than on a new first mortgage. This is because a second mortgage holder's claim on the property comes after the claim secured by the first mortgage. You may pay a higher rate for your $5,000, $10,000, or even $20,000 mortgage. However, you get a lower rate on the first mortgage. You are still better off than if you got a single first mortgage for the full amount at current mortgage rates.

■ *CAUTION NOTE: Sometimes sellers want more interest on a second mortgage when they allow you to assume the existing, first mortgage.*

You're not always permitted to assume a conventional mortgage loan. In the late 1960s and early 1970s, banks got wise to takeovers and assumptions. They began putting clauses in their mortgage agreements to prevent a new buyer from taking over existing financing. However, many older mortgages can still be assumed. And even newer loans with higher rates can be taken over with the bank's permission.

■ *CAUTION NOTE: Banks often have clauses preventing takeovers in their mortgage agreements.*

■ *KEY POINT: Many older loans can still be taken over.*

THE TRADITIONAL SECOND MORTGAGE

We've already talked about second mortgages with other loans. They are often what make other loans work. For most buyers, the second mortgage helps make up the difference between the down payment and the first mortgage.

■ *KEY POINT: A second mortgage is often what makes seller financing work.*

The first mortgage is first in the line of security in case of default and later foreclosure on the loan. The payback on a first mortgage is made before the second, third, or other mortgages. The second mortgage, since it is subordinate to the first, often has a slightly higher interest rate due to this extra risk. No set rule applies; often, if the seller is anxious to sell, the rate might be slightly less than current rates.

■ *CAUTION NOTE: The higher rate of a second mortgage is commensurate with the extra risk involved.*

Sometimes, a considerable down payment must be made on assuming a loan. The existing loan might be only 30% or 40% of the selling price. You might only have 10% or 20% as a down payment. The difference should be negotiated as a second mortgage with the seller.

■ *KEY POINT: Assuming a second mortgage often requires a larger down payment.*

In most cases, the seller—depending on his or her motivation—is willing to give the second mortgage on an assumption. If the seller doesn't need the cash to purchase another house, he or she can benefit from the interest, particularly if the rate is more than he or she could get in bonds or certificates of deposit. After all, the seller shouldn't be worried about the value of a second mortgage since it's secured by the property itself, and he or she has set the selling price. If anyone believes in the property's value, hence the second mortgage, it should be the seller.

■ *KEY POINT: A reasonable interest rate on a second mortgage is usually more than the seller can get elsewhere.*

Even when the seller does not take the first mortgage, the second mortgage is a likely alternative. For example, when your new 80% bank loan isn't enough because you only have 15% to put down, it's not uncommon for the seller to help with that extra 5%. If the property sells for $150,000, the $7,500 the seller loans you—let's say for five years with quarterly payments at an interest rate no more than the bank is charging—can be a real help in getting the right property.

■ *KEY POINT: Rates for second mortgages given by sellers are usually equal to or a point above the bank's rate.*

A seller will often want a second mortgage to balloon after a few years so he or she can get the money out. The seller doesn't usually want to lend the money for as long as a bank. To keep payments lower, however, long-term plans in which the balance comes due in a shorter period are negotiated.

■ *KEY POINT: The ballooning of the balance must be prepared for but keeps you from being overwhelmed with large payments.*

There's no difference between buying an investment or commercial property with a second mortgage and buying a house. In fact, the businessperson is likely to be more familiar with holding a mortgage and thereby will be more willing to give a larger amount than a homeowner.

The owner of a business property may live in the same community. He or she may feel more secure in holding the mortgage on a property that can be seen and inspected.

■ *KEY POINT: Owners of investment property often feel more secure in giving a second mortgage.*

A builder's new house or condominium can often be bought with secondary financing. The builder may already have arranged for attractive bank financing at below-market rates and as further encouragement makes up a 5% to 10% difference in a second mortgage.

■ *KEY POINT: Builders often plan to help buyers of new homes by giving second mortgages.*

Again, in negotiating any mortgage, particularly with a private party, make sure that you have a competent attorney to do the necessary legal work. This might consist of a title search to make sure there are no other encumbrances on the property you are buying. You also want your lawyer to make sure that any written agreement is specific and clearly understandable. The lawyer will also see to it that the mortgage is recorded in the local Registry of Deeds.

Because of the extra legal work in helping to arrange seller financing, expect your attorney's fee to be somewhat higher.

■ *CAUTION NOTE: Always consult with an attorney when arranging secondary financing.*

Any time you buy with financing provided by the seller, the provisions for doing so are included in the purchase offer. So, when the offer is accepted, the financing is, too. This provision need be nothing more than a sentence within the offer form. In most legal jurisdictions, formal papers detailing the actual terms of the mortgage agreement are drawn up by the lawyers 10 to 14 days after both parties have signed the offer form. In this more formal purchase and sale agreement, the financing provision may be spelled out in more detail. However, it must reflect the basic provision contained in the offer form.

■ *KEY POINT: Seller financing is negotiated with the purchase price and terms.*

Second mortgages are the most frequent form of financing help given by a seller to a buyer in the United States. Estimates are that over half of all residential and business sales include secondary financing.

THE WRAPAROUND MORTGAGE AND HOW IT WORKS

Wraparound or all-inclusive mortgages are mortgages taken back by the seller or institutional lender with the existing financing. They are a form of second mortgage; a first mortgage is already on the property and the wraparound is in a secondary position. It is sometimes called an overriding trustee or overriding mortgage.

■ *KEY POINT: Wraparound mortgages include existing and new financing.*

How does a wraparound mortgage work? Here's one scenario. The seller of a small apartment building has an existing loan with a balance of $40,000 at 8.5% and 20 years left to pay. He agrees to sell it to you for $80,000. You will put up $15,000 in cash, leaving $25,000 to be financed. You could refinance the first mortgage of $40,000 to a higher amount, but you likely would pay a much higher interest rate. In addition, money is tight, and the bank isn't willing to extend itself beyond the existing $40,000. Another possibility would be to assume the existing loan of $40,000 and have the seller carry back a second mortgage for the remaining $25,000.

A better alternative is to construct a wraparound mortgage. For example, the seller agrees to a mortgage of $65,000 at a rate between the old rate of 8.5% and the current rate of 12% for commercial property charged by the banks—10%, for instance. In the written agreement detailing the provisions, a clause will state this mortgage includes the unpaid balance of the existing first mortgage and that the seller is still responsible for this debt. He must make payments on the existing $40,000 mortgage at 8.5% from the payment you make to him on the $65,000 mortgage at 10%.

■ *KEY POINT: In a wraparound mortgage, the seller is often still responsible for paying the existing loan.*

The advantage to the seller is the 1.5% he makes as profit, plus a full 10% on the $25,000 difference. As the buyer, you benefit too. Although you don't get the 8.5% on the existing $40,000—it is 10% overall—you've saved some, considering the current market rate. You have also avoided any prepayment penalties that might have been charged by an institutional lender.

■ *KEY POINT: Wraparounds save interest and points.*

The wraparound can also be an excellent technique when the existing mortgage has a low interest rate and is nonassumable. Let's say an $85,000 property has a 10-year-old first mortgage with a balance of $40,000 at 6% interest. You, the buyer, are willing to put down a $15,000 deposit. That leaves a balance of $30,000. Instead of the seller giving you a straight second mortgage for this $30,000, as might occur if the first $40,000 could be assumed, the seller gives a wraparound, an overall mortgage that includes the first mortgage and a hypothetical (the amount of the normal second) second totaling $70,000.

The incentive for you is that the overall interest rate for the wraparound is less than current bank rates. If the current fixed rate is 10% and you and the seller settle on an overall interest rate of 8%, the seller benefits because he's making two points of interest over the old loan. This is better for him than if you obtained a new mortgage for $40,000 and he then gave you a second mortgage for the remaining $30,000, though the second mortgage might carry an interest rate closer to the current rate.

■ *KEY POINT: Wraparounds can also be used to take over existing nonassumable loans.*

The seller, then, is better off by negotiating a wraparound mortgage, even if he receives less than current rates. You benefit because you can't take over the existing mortgage but can get the mortgage money you need at favorable rates.

■ *KEY POINT: Both buyer and seller can benefit by negotiating a wraparound.*

The major difficulty with a wraparound or all-inclusive mortgage lies in its limitation in mortgage agreements that lack a "due and payable" clause against the property; the clause may cause trouble if the mortgage is taken over by someone else. Solution: Hold the deed in escrow until the loan is paid off. Also, it's always possible the bank might waive this clause and allow the loan to stand.

■ *CAUTION NOTE: It is difficult to "wraparound" all nonassumable loans.*

Wraparounds work when it is difficult to negotiate the price of the property with the seller but the seller will allow you to take over the existing financing, which may have a low rate.

WHEN YOU WANT A BOND FOR DEED

A bond for deed is another way to get around an institutional lender's nonassumable "due on sale" clause in a mortgage agreement. In a bond for deed sale, the property is held in escrow by a title company or lawyer. It is not recorded, since this would trigger the nonassumable clause within the mortgage. You, as the buyer make payments to the previous owner, who, in turn, gives these payments to the bank. The mortgage is held under the seller's name. A down payment or second mortgage is given to the seller.

■ *KEY POINT: A bond for deed transaction involves seller financing with the deed held in escrow.*

■ *KEY POINT: A bond for deed gets around nonassumable loan clauses.*

As with many existing mortgages, there may be less than a 50% balance left and an excellent interest rate that is desirable to take over. The disadvantage, however minor, is that the title is not in your name. Therefore, you must have legal assurances from the seller that the money you give him or her will be used to pay off the loan.

■ *CAUTION NOTE: Gain assurance from the seller that your payments will be used to pay the existing mortgage.*

As with any sale where the seller gives the financing, the bond for deed is negotiated on the same offer form as the selling price. You get an instantaneous loan acceptance without the need for a separate financial proposal.

■ *KEY POINT: A bond for deed sale involves instant financing.*

WHEN A LEASE WITH OPTION MAKES SENSE

Another way to take over an existing loan is to lease the property with an option to take over formal ownership in the future. You pay all expenses, including the mortgage, while gaining full use of the property. A favored technique for many buyers of investment property, it can also work in taking over a private residence.

■ *KEY POINT: A lease with option gives control while deferring the actual sale.*

Technically, you only lease the property, but when you have an option to buy you have much more authority and control than the average tenant. It is a way to take over a property with no money down. You don't have to give the seller any down payment, although you may give money for the option. You pay a negotiated monthly rent. If it's an income property, this fee will be based on how much money is left over after you have collected the tenants' rent and paid all operating expenses, including the mortgage.

■ *CAUTION NOTE: You may pay the seller money for option rights.*

All the operating costs, including the bank payments, will in most cases be made directly by you; this assures that they are being made and also shows your control. The option to purchase often cites a time by which you must buy; it might also be open-ended. You might not have to assume ownership until you wish to transfer the property to another buyer, or if you wish, you may not purchase at all.

■ *KEY POINT: Sometimes, the time to take up the option is not established, allowing you to sell to another buyer.*

It's the easiest way to take over a mortgage. Even if the loan is nonassumable, the lender cannot call it, since the original owner still officially has the title. You are simply leasing the property and making payments directly to the bank for the holder of the title. If you and the seller agree, the deed could be signed over to you and held in escrow.

■ *KEY POINT: A lease with option is an easy way to take over the responsibility of a nonassumable mortgage.*

Here's how a lease with option might work. You agree to lease with an option of $200,000 an eight-unit apartment building. The existing loan, at a favorable 7.5% (commercial property), has been paid down to $110,000. It was originally for 20 years. Since the present owners have owned the property for 10 years, the loan has 10 more years to go. If you had to refinance this $110,000 (though you could possibly get more money than that, say, up to $150,000), you might have to pay for commercial property as much as 11% to 13% or more in interest.

You negotiate with the sellers a rent that approximates the amount paid if you had a second mortgage with them. If you give them a $10,000 "down payment" as a sign that you will perform on your option, that leaves a difference from the $110,000 first mortgage of $80,000. If this $80,000 were invested at 10% for 10 years, you would earn $12,686 annually, $1,057 monthly. This amount, then is the rent you pay the sellers under the terms of your lease. It is constructed as a second mortgage, so should you take over the property before the end of the 10 years, the balance would become due.

This arrangement allows you to take over the property and not take title until a future time. The $10,000 down payment could be handled as a security deposit, an amount guaranteeing that you will follow through with the terms of the lease. In many areas, when a lease runs more than 5 or 10 years, it must be recorded in the local county Registry of Deeds as a formal document.

■ *KEY POINT: Long-term leases are often recorded in the local Registry of Deeds.*

Another way the lease with option could work is to send all monies due on mortgages to the seller, who will make the payments. Or, you may negotiate with the seller for you to make those payments directly to the bank, thus assuring that the funds are being deposited.

■ *KEY POINT: Payment on existing mortgages can be made by you through the seller or directly.*

The disadvantage in leasing is that you are not the owner of record and cannot get depreciation deductions that accrue with the ownership of investment property (more on this in Chapter 11). However, IRS regulations imply that long-term leasing is like ownership; if so stipulated in your agreement with the seller, you may be eligible for these deductions. Check with your accountant.

■ *CAUTION NOTE: Leasing does not normally qualify you for depreciation deductions.*

Whether you're a tenant or an owner of an income property, all costs (property taxes, utility charges, snow removal, etc.) are deductible as ordinary expenses. The mortgage payments you make are the seller's but are deductible for you if based on rent that must be paid to the seller.

■ *KEY POINT: Under most circumstances, business deductions can only be taken by the person paying the bills.*

The lease with option is an excellent technique in taking over a property—the bank is not involved. The investment is minimal, the closing is deferred, and most of the benefits of ownership can be enjoyed in the meantime.

A VARIATION: MANAGEMENT AGREEMENT WITH OPTION (MAO)

Here's another way to take over a property and defer formal financing until later. Like leasing with an option, it's a method for you to get control of a property with no down payment and no financial negotiations with the bank.

The management agreement with option is a technique for taking over larger investment properties that require management skill. It's not normally used to take possession of a house. Most sellers require cash or a firm commitment on a first or second mortgage before they sell. However, if the seller is willing, particularly if he or she is an absentee businessperson, doesn't have a ready buyer for cash, and wishes to be out from under the ongoing financial responsibility, an MAO is possible.

■ *CAUTION NOTE: A management agreement with option is not normally used to take over single-family houses.*

In the management agreement with option, you take over the property immediately by virtue of an agreement with the seller to manage the property. In it, you assume full control, and continue to do so until you take title. The timetable is specified in your option.

■ *KEY POINT: A management agreement with option gives you full control over the property and tenants.*

Included in the management agreement and option are guarantees assuring that some day the property will be yours. All you need to do is be able to finance it at some agreed-on time. First, the option to take over the property at a set time in the future is guaranteed. Second, the deed must be signed over to you but held unrecorded in your lawyer's office. Third, you must give some guarantee of performance to the seller, such as a down payment or promissory note. The purchase price is based on the current market.

■ *KEY POINT: MAOs consist of an option, escrowed deed, and promissory guarantee.*

Fourth, since you may invest money in the property, you want to protect yourself in case of the seller's bankruptcy, since technically he or she owns the property. To do this, you negotiate a second mortgage from the seller to you to cover your down payment (if any) and any additional amount of future equity that will protect your effort. This second mortgage only takes effect in the event of and at the seller's foreclosure (such as a sheriff's sale). This mortgage is recorded. The idea is to protect you from a worst-case scenario. The prospect may sound unlikely, but the paperwork is essential in case of litigation.

■ *KEY POINT: A second mortgage, from the seller to you, effective only if the seller is foreclosured, protects your equity and effort.*

Should the worst happen to the seller, endangering the property you now control, your recorded second mortgage takes precedence over other debts. In addition, you may choose to record the deed and take formal possession, depending on your lawyer's advice.

Why bother with an MAO? The answer is obvious. How else could you take over a large property with little or no down payment? Furthermore, mortgage money may be tight or interest rates high, making it otherwise difficult for you to purchase.

■ *KEY POINT: Like the lease with option, the MAO gives you control.*

A management agreement with option works on an investment property (apartments or commercial buildings) when institutional money has dried up. You're taking over the property and deferring the negotiation of formal financing until money is more available and rates are better.

■ *KEY POINT: An MAO defers financing until mortgage money is more available and rates are lower.*

In addition, the equity of your property will increase so much in several years that when you go to the bank to get financing, you won't have to put up any additional funds. This future but cheaper money makes it easy to pay off the seller.

■ *KEY POINT: Larger equity and cheaper dollars in the future make the past selling price easier to pay.*

You may ask where the seller's money comes from. Until the actual closing, you will be making payments to the seller based on the criteria you have negotiated in the management agreement. You may also have negotiated a second mortgage that you are paying off. What the seller gets are funds that are over operating expenses and mortgage payments. You might negotiate to give him or her any funds that are left after you have paid the mortgages and taken a management fee for yourself.

■ *KEY POINT: In an MAO, a second mortgage may be used as an option or down payment.*

This may appear complicated, but it is not. Once explained to the seller, he or she can be most amenable—particularly if motivated to sell but having difficulty in a climate of tight money and high rates.

■ *KEY POINT: An MAO works best for a highly motivated seller of investment or commercial property.*

This is an excellent way to take over a property where an existing mortgage cannot be renegotiated favorably or cannot be assumed. It is, in effect, a way to bypass a nonassumable mortgage.

EXCHANGING PROPERTY

Exchanging property is similar to the barter system of ancient days. It usually involves investment property. Two owners can trade their investments, and if those investments are equal in value—what is known as a "like-kind" exchange—under a special provision of the Internal Revenue Code, the owners can avoid paying tax on the gain from the sale/exchange at the time of transfer.

■ *KEY POINT: Investors can defer tax when exchanging "like-kind" property.*

Avoiding taxes is not the only reason professional investors exchange property. Another is to keep trading up, getting a larger and larger property. The previous property is used as equity for the newer, larger one. All this can be done without having to sell the first, or exchanged, property and triggering taxes.

■ *KEY POINT: Exchanging property is an ideal way to trade up to a larger investment.*

When trading up, the difference in value is usually compensated for by the assumption of an existing and larger mortgage. This could be a new first mortgage combined with a second mortgage. In some cases, cash may be used to even the deal.

■ *KEY POINT: In an exchange, only minimal cash may be needed to take over a larger property.*

This technique is thought by many to be a clear path to making a fortune in real estate. The exchange reduces tax consequences and often the need for additional large down payments. Some investors trade properties several times in a 5-year span. Others may do so once in 10 years. No matter how often a person trades, it is an ideal way to pyramid equity.

■ *KEY POINT: Exchanging "like-kind" property builds rapid equity and defers taxes.*

There is no tax consequence on the sale of one home and the purchase of another in like-kind exchanges. In most other cases, the owner defers tax on the first residence if this new property (it must be the same or higher value than the one before) is bought within two years of the sale. This is a special provision in the tax law for residential homes only.

■ *KEY POINT: In trading up homes, taxes can be deferred if the transfer takes place within two years.*

■ *CAUTION NOTE: To defer taxes in an exchange of investment property, the transfer must be at the same time.*

The reason the exchange technique must be used for investment property is that no deferral is allowed on an actual sale, though something of equal value and utility is bought. So the IRS allows a tax deferment when a "like-kind" exchange occurs.

■ *CAUTION NOTE: When a nonexchange or straight sale occurs, tax on the gain must be paid during the year of the sale.*

Only through the exchange of property, which should always be done with a knowledgeable attorney, can you defer taxable gain until you sell the last property you exchanged. Years later, when you sell the seventh or eighth exchanged property, you finally have to pay the tax. However, with the diminishing value of the dollar, it still is better for you to pay later.

■ *CAUTION NOTE: Exchanges should only be tried with knowledgeable professionals.*

■ *KEY POINT: Many properties can be exchanged during an extended span of ownership.*

THE EASY WAY TO SELL YOURSELF TO THE SELLER

To get financing from sellers, you must first understand their motivations. They have the property, and you wish to buy it.

Now you need to know why it is for sale. Do they simply want to buy something else if the right property comes along? Or, must they move because of a job change? Or, is the small apartment building you're looking at owned by people who want to buy a larger investment? Or, have the sellers owned the property for some years and lost their depreciation advantage? Or, are financial obligations, such as sending children to college or paying doctors' bills, the reason?

A seller who must move or raise cash quickly is highly motivated. You will therefore have an easier time negotiating.

■ *KEY POINT:* *The seller's motivation is the key to financing.*

What are some other motivations of sellers? The seller may have an expanding family and need a larger house with more bedrooms. Often, a divorce will cause a property to be sold. A commercial or investment building may need repairs that are beyond the capability and funds of the present owner. These are just some of the reasons owners want to sell. The stronger the seller's motivation, the easier you can negotiate favorable terms to take back financing or otherwise tailor your purchase. If the seller is not sufficiently motivated, you cannot get financing this way.

■ *KEY POINT:* *The stronger the seller's motivation, the more financing help you can get.*

■ *CAUTION NOTE:* *Without strong motivation, the seller may not be willing to finance.*

HOW TO AVOID THE RISKS IN SELLER FINANCING

The key to real estate success, whether the vehicle is a home, investment, parcel of land, or a second home, is financing. Some superior opportunities are available in seller financing. Once you know the seller's motivation, you can construct the most advantageous financial terms for you and the seller. This brings up the following point: There's no reason to do business with the seller unless you can get a much better rate and terms than are obtainable from a bank.

■ *KEY POINT: Finance with the seller for a better deal.*

Buyers often look at a selling price and feel they've overpaid if a bank doesn't approve the property's value and finance it. This is a fallacy. A bank never confirms the selling price of a property for you.

■ *CAUTION NOTE: Don't look to a bank for expert advice on property values.*

The bank is unlikely to grant a loan if you overpay, but banks are not value experts. They often base their loan on your ability to make payments and other intangible factors such as whether the market is expanding and whether they'll make a profit. When they're anxious to loan money, they don't look closely at value.

■ *CAUTION NOTE: Banks often overlook property value in granting a loan if they can profit on your payments.*

If they feel you can meet payments and they will profit with interest rates and points, they're likely to extend the loan. That's not any protection against paying too much.

How then do you know you aren't paying more than you should? The answer is twofold. First, in buying any property, you should look at several comparable properties in the neighboring area. With a real estate agent squiring you to different houses, you will get a sense of what properties are worth by comparing such qualities as neighborhood, size, and construction.

■ *KEY POINT: Assure yourself of value by comparison shopping.*

Values for houses of similar style and type in the same area don't vary by more than a few thousand dollars. And, that range is probably based on extras such as swimming pools and garages.

■ *KEY POINT: The values of similar properties in similar neighborhoods won't vary much.*

The value of an income property depends as much on the income it produces after expenses as on its bricks and mortar.

■ *KEY POINT: Much of the value of investment property is based on net income after expenses.*

The second and more important aspect about paying too much is the financing itself. In part, the value of real estate is based on the cost of mortgage financing. Specifically, high interest rates depress prices; conversely, low rates inflate prices slightly.

■ *KEY POINT: Contrary to popular opinion, the value of real estate is predicated, in part, on the availability of financing.*

■ *CAUTION NOTE: When money is tight and rates are high, property values become depressed.*

Institutional lenders set the "market"; that is, the particular interest rate being charged has a direct effect on prices.

What does this mean to you? It means if you negotiate two or three percentage points off the going bank rate in a mortgage with a seller, your net cost for the deal is less than that of someone who got a bank mortgage.

■ *KEY POINT: Any time you negotiate a lower-than-normal interest rate, you lower the overall cost of the property.*

This doesn't mean you should pay more for the property to get a financing deal with a seller. However, it does give you a margin of protection. If a seller provides you a loan at 6.5% interest when the going rate is 9.5%, you are benefiting by 3% a year.

This can add up to real savings, a big reason for you to try to get seller financing. Some investors don't even consider a property if the seller won't offer a large amount of financing. It's not that they don't want to do business with a bank; they just want a better rate for their loan and to avoid origination points and prepayment penalties.

■ *KEY POINT: Some investment strategies call for financing through sellers only.*

The key to taking the risk out of seller financing lies in the motivation of the seller. The higher that motivation, the better deal you will negotiate. Any margin of savings over current interest rates makes your investment cost that much less.

■ *KEY POINT: Financing with a motivated seller takes the gamble out of buying property.*

In Chapter 10, you will learn how to finance a property with little or no money down.

WHAT TO DO WHEN YOU HAVE LITTLE OR NO CASH TO PUT DOWN 10

A few people who should know better—seminar givers, real estate counselors, investment advertisers, writers of real estate books—try to undermine our common sense and convince us that property can be commonly bought with no money down. Something for nothing! They tell us we can buy $100,000 or $1,000,000 properties without spending a dime. They should know better.

■ *CAUTION NOTE: Property can seldom be bought with no money down.*

As with many investment schemes—opportunities, as we learn in seminars—an element of truth exists. Occasionally, we can buy expensive property with little or no money down. Even a mortgage on a home can reach 90% to 95% of the selling price, reducing the down payment.

■ *KEY POINT: Often, you can buy property with 5% to 10% down.*

Although nothing is inherently wrong with a no-money-down deal, there are two stumbling blocks. The first is finding an owner who will agree to sell property to someone who is unable or unwilling to invest anything. The second is that a property can be difficult to pay for when financing is extremely high. Most income properties won't pay for themselves when fully financed.

■ *CAUTION NOTE: Obstacles to no-money-down deals include lack of a motivated seller and large mortgage payments.*

HOW TO GET STARTED WITH NO CASH

Despite these opening words of caution, we're going to examine various viable options for investing little or no cash as a down payment. There's no mystery about it. To start, you need a highly motivated seller who is willing to give you a purchase money mortgage for the entire purchase price. Alternatively, the seller might add secondary financing to make up the difference between a bank's first mortgage and the selling price.

■ *KEY POINT: Find a seller willing to arrange a no-money-down deal.*

Another alternative is to borrow the down payment from a third party, such as a commercial bank.

Nearly all techniques for buying with no money down involve instant money—mortgage money given by the seller. In most cases, therefore, you will need to negotiate with the seller, who will either give you the complete mortgage or extra financing beyond what the bank will loan.

■ *KEY POINT: Most no-money-down deals involve help from the seller.*

BUYING WITH NO MONEY DOWN

One way to do this, without requiring the cooperation of the seller, is to borrow the down payment from a commercial bank, as a personal loan. Banks are often willing to lend $5,000 on a signature, possibly more to individuals with a good financial history and the means to pay back the loan. Frequently, they don't ask any questions about why you are borrowing the money. If they do, it is only out of concern that the loan is to serve a useful purpose. And, what could be more useful than the purchase of real estate?

■ *KEY POINT: Commercial banks can often help out with personal, unsecured loans.*

Commercial banks can be found in most communities. These banks loan money to small businesses for inventory and goods; loan money to individuals for major purchases, such as cars; and handle checking accounts. They often grant your loan request the same day, if not within 24 hours.

A more common way for investors to buy with no money down involves considerable help from the seller. It usually works best on investment or commercial property, since it requires a strongly motivated seller.

Just because a seller must dispose of a property, doesn't mean it has any insurmountable physical or economic problems. The seller may have held it too long or perhaps is just tired of dealing with tenants or is unable to make needed improvements.

■ *KEY POINT: Some sellers want to divest themselves of a property for intangible reasons.*

Most sellers of homes are unable to give 100% financing; some cannot give any at all. They may be moving to another area and need all the cash they can get to buy a new home. Or perhaps a couple is divorcing and find it impractical to hold a mortgage from a new buyer jointly.

■ *CAUTION NOTE: Not all sellers can help with financing, especially if they need all available cash to buy a new property.*

However, a businessperson with an investment is in a better position to negotiate the large mortgage necessary for extensive financing.

■ *KEY POINT:*   *Businesspersons owning income property are prime candi-*
dates to give extensive financing.

Let's look at a no-money-down purchase where the seller
makes up the difference between the new first mortgage and
the selling price. The seller makes a deal with you for a price of
$230,000 on a 12-unit apartment building. He presently has a
mortgage of $80,000 on it. You tell him you want an all-cash, no-
money-down deal. He is highly motivated to sell and knows
you could be a better manager of the property than he has been.
He knows you would be a good risk, but he still needs to re-
cover some cash from the deal.

You can't just take over the $80,000 mortgage and have the
seller give you a second mortgage for the difference. He needs
some cash or he won't sell it to you. Through negotiations, he
agrees to the deal if he can put $40,000 in his pocket. You start
by getting a $120,000 first mortgage at 11% interest. The old rate
was 9%, and the bank is glad to raise its rate. Further, the mortgage officers are pleased their exposure is only around 50% of
the property's value. They approve the loan the same day you
present it to them.

Now the seller will get his $40,000 from the difference be-
tween the new mortgage of $120,000 and the $80,000 he must
pay off on his old loan. He then gives you a second mortgage of
$110,000, which, added to the new mortgage, equals the selling
price. Since you accommodated his interest in getting cash via a
new first mortgage, you negotiate with him a modest rate for
his second mortgage: 9%, or two percentage points less than
what you must pay on the first mortgage.

Although a seller with no existing mortgage could give you a
whole mortgage, this is uncommon—most investment properties carry existing financing.

■ *CAUTION NOTE:*   *A seller can't give you a first mortgage on a property*
with existing financing.

Almost any no-cash-down deal requires a motivated seller
who is willing to take less cash and give you considerable

secondary financing. As the seminars tell you, find a seller who is distressed.

Psychology can help in a no-money-down sale. Most sellers are more interested in getting their asking price than they are in how the financing will work and how much cash they will get right away. This motivation may encourage the seller to deal in the $230,000 on paper rather than with someone who offers $210,000 in cash.

■ *KEY POINT: Sellers often opt for a higher selling price on paper over a lesser offer in cash.*

This may not appear to make sense. As we saw in Chapter 9, mortgages, that is, money pledged on paper, are worth less than their face value. Generally, we would rather have cash in hand than a promise to receive it in the future—unless a healthy interest rate is attached to mollify our reluctance.

■ *KEY POINT: The interest rate compensates for the difference between the value of cash and a mortgage.*

Sellers, especially distressed ones, are emotional negotiators, however, and once they have a fixed selling price in mind, they'd rather compromise on anything else before this amount. Many buyers take advantage of this tendency by offering the asking price or close to it, but on their terms. Often, the only way you can meet a seller's price is to have much, if not all, of the transaction in notes and mortgages.

■ *KEY POINT: Start negotiating a no-money-down deal by offering the full price.*

The problem is that the entire, capital amount of the property is on paper, increasing your indebtedness dramatically. If it's an apartment building, you may be worried about whether the rent money will cover monthly payments. Whether it's one mortgage or four smaller mortgages to as many different people, you will have a financial obligation of whopping proportions.

■ *CAUTION NOTE: Rental income may not cover the immense payments required by no-money-down transactions.*

This doesn't mean these deals won't work; both the financing and the operating of the property can work. If it's an income property, look closely to make sure there's enough money from rents or be prepared to add the difference each month.

WHEN IT'S BEST TO ADD A LITTLE

To avoid high payments, make some down payment. Any amount will help reduce those monthly payments to manageable proportions. A 100% financed deal in which every dollar beyond operating expenses goes out to meet mortgage indebtedness can lead to an unhealthy investment. Even if you get a personal loan at a bank to help with the down payment, you still must pay it back. If you have any cash for a down payment, it's money you don't have to come up with later.

Getting an unusually good deal from a seller might indicate a problem property. His or her problem might become your problem. If the property has deteriorated to the point that a large investment is needed to keep it going, then you're defeating the purpose of putting no money down. You're going to need a lot of money to make these repairs. The community or state, for example, may have demanded that the owner comply with new zoning or health and safety regulations. If such repairs involve a large and expensive upgrading of the property, the named violations could make the owner become a seller.

Also keep in mind that at the beginning of a loan, interest is the bulk of the monthly payment. An actual reduction of the loan balance, with a corresponding increase in equity doesn't occur until years later.

■ *CAUTION NOTE: An anxious seller often indicates a distressed property needing capital expenditures.*

■ *CAUTION NOTE: Having to meet new zoning or health and safety regulations can drive an owner to sell.*

In a problem-property sale, you—more often than not—are
going to be the one who pays. Either the seller does the work
and you pay a higher sale price, or you take over and spend the
money yourself. Not that this is all bad. It's just that no-money-
down deals often involve damaged properties. Your awareness,
however, will be your protection when you are offered a no-
money-down deal on a $150,000 property that's in bad shape—
you can figure the deal at twice the price.

■ *KEY POINT: A distressed property can also mean you can negotiate a
good deal.*

These distressed properties can frequently be good deals,
but you must be knowledgeable and prepared to handle them
financially. Sometimes when you put down some money, as little as a 5% down payment, you can get a much better property
than one with 100% financing.

EXTRA HELP FROM LENDERS AND SELLERS

The recent dampened economy has made it tough for many borrowers to come up with the cash to pay loan closing costs. Some
lenders have stepped in to help.

Routinely, you as a borrower will need the cash to cover origination charges and costs for appraisal, inspection, title insurance, legal services, and recording fees. These expenses can
average as much as 5% of the loan amount, or about $4,000 on an
$80,000 loan.

Some lenders are offering to pay all or some of those costs in
exchange for a slightly higher rate of interest on the loan. For
moderate-income or first-time buyers, some lenders even waive
the added interest charges. Sellers have also begun to help with
closing expenses to make their homes more salable although

they may request a slightly higher price in reciprocation. If you do wish to negotiate with the seller, include closing costs in your initial offer.

■ *KEY POINT:* *Some lenders and sellers will pay all or part of closing costs.*

A typical lender helping with closing costs might work like this: If you are willing to make a down payment of at least 10%, the lender will pay most closing costs and origination charges in return for adding about 0.75% to the interest rate. This is only an additional $50 per month, but on an $80,000, 25-year loan it can add up to $15,000.

■ *CAUTION NOTE:* *The extra interest rate charge for including closing costs can be expensive over time.*

Assuming your closing fees might amount to $4,000 on an $80,000 loan, or $5,000 on a $100,000 loan, this approach allows you to put that extra money toward the down payment, thereby reducing the amount of mortgage needed. Monthly payments will not be larger, even at the higher interest rate because the loan will be smaller. Furthermore, you would have additional equity in the home instead of spending the money on closing fees.

FIFTEEN WAYS TO BUY WITH LITTLE OR NO CASH

In this section, we'll discuss 15 ways in which you can buy a property with little or no money down.

Seller Financing for Low Down Payment

If the seller helps finance, you lessen your down payment. You often get a better deal from the seller than a bank. Neither a conventional nor an ARM loan can match the benefits of seller financing.

Instead of 20% down, you make deals for only 5% or 10% down. The key is the seller's motivation. If it is strong enough, you can get a purchase money mortgage or a secondary mortgage for most of the selling price.

To encourage the seller, offer a higher rate of interest than the bank charges. If you don't have the cash, this often gets the property you want. The seller needn't be in dire straits to want to benefit from a little extra interest. This is particularly true if you show good faith by presenting some down payment.

■ *KEY POINT: With the seller's help, you can reduce your down payment.*

Using Other Assets as Security

A blanket mortgage, also called an overlapping mortgage or trust deed, covers two or more separate parcels of property. Putting up a property you already own assures you of getting a maximum amount of financing. With the risk spread over two or more properties, the blanket mortgage gives the lender some safety.

Blanket or overlapping mortgages also work if you get secondary financing from the seller. You pledge a second property, perhaps a house or business investment, as additional security for the second mortgage.

Either way, a blanket mortgage gives the bank or seller a margin of security, thereby guaranteeing you maximum financing.

■ *KEY POINT: A blanket mortgage overlapping other property gives the security needed to get a loan.*

Borrow on Other Property

A typical way to raise money is to borrow on property you presently own. This is not unlike the blanket mortgage.

Whether you want a second home or an investment, you can refinance your present mortgage. Sometimes, the bank that holds the existing mortgage will add another mortgage as a second loan. This gives you the money necessary for a down payment on another property—without taking any cash out of your pocket.

Naturally, you must already own a property with some minimal equity. However, if you have paid a mortgage on a home or small investment for several years, there should be enough equity for a bank to accept the property as additional security.

■ *KEY POINT: Extending your existing mortgage or borrowing a second raises the down payment for a new property.*

Enticing the Seller with Profit Sharing

If you have little or no down payment, promise the seller a share in either the property's income or future appreciation. Big banks and insurance companies do this in financing huge developments, so why not between private parties? The seller is more likely to provide full financing if there's hope for profit later.

Even banks have programs called shared-appreciation loans in which, for a minimal interest rate, they share in profits of the future sale of the property.

■ *KEY POINT: In a no-money-down deal, entice the seller with a share of the future profit.*

When Exchanging Property Can Be to Your Advantage

Bartering what we own is an age-old way of transferring assets, and there is nothing new about exchanging properties. We occasionally exchange homes and investors exchange income or commercial property, often in intricate two-, three-, and four-way deals. Each time we do so, we use our equity in the property being exchanged as leverage in getting new financing.

Exchanging property has special tax benefits for investors. If you sold an investment property, you would pay tax on the profit in the year of that sale—a profit based on your selling price minus any transaction costs and remaining tax basis (the original price of the property plus capital improvements minus depreciation taken). When you make an exchange of properties of equal value, you don't pay this tax. You defer it by the exchange, transferring your tax basis into the new property.

A similar transaction occurs when you transfer your tax basis into a second residence. However, with a personal residence, you don't have to make an actual exchange; you can sell and have up to 24 months to buy the new home. And, as with investment property, you defer the tax on the profit.

You can keep repeating this process, but only if the property is a private residence. As long as you keep buying a property of the same or higher value, you can defer the tax on each gain until you sell your final property without reinvesting.

However, for investment property, exchange is the only way to avoid this tax. You can't sell and find something else—the second property must be part of the exchange. Depending on the value of the properties, however, you benefit by reducing the need for a large down payment.

The combination of minimal down payment and low taxes makes this technique popular for professional real estate investors. These investors even form clubs that actively seek owners with whom they can make exchanges.

■ *KEY POINT:* *When you exchange one property for another, your present equity is used as the down payment.*

Government Veterans Administration Loans

If you are a veteran, you can purchase a home with no down payment if the home's appraisal is within acceptable limits.

These so-called GI loans are fraught with paperwork and constantly changing regulations. Banks, which are involved in lending the money, shy away from these loans when the stated rate at which they must lend the money is less than that of their fixed-rate loans. The banks do, however, get a guarantee from the government that protects them in case of default.

If you qualify, you can buy an approved home with no down payment.

■ *KEY POINT: If you qualify for a GI loan, you can buy with no down payment.*

Federal Housing Administration Guarantee

FHA loans, like GI loans, are not made by the government. Institutional lenders loan the money, and the FHA insures them against loss. The rates vary with market conditions.

The advantage is that the loan payment may be less than with a conventional loan; often the loans can be up to 97% of the property's appraised value. The FHA has an intricate appraisal process with high standards to protect you from paying an excessive price.

■ *KEY POINT: Although time consuming, an FHA loan can reduce the down payment to 3%.*

Private Mortgage Insurance

Privately owned companies, often branches or subsidiaries of large insurance companies, are active in guaranteeing mortgages. Guarantees have become popular with banks in the past decade. They take the burden off the bank in case of default.

Here's how it works. In addition to the regular interest, a borrower pays an extra 0.25% to 0.50% in interest as a fee for insurance to a private insurer in addition to the regular interest. In case of default, this insurance company will reimburse the lending bank a portion of the loan, thus protecting the bank against an entire loss. The bank is therefore in a safer position to lend a higher percentage of loan to property value—90% rather than 80%—than would normally be the case.

Some banks, with a guarantee from a private mortgage company, will allow you to buy a home with only 5% down.

■ *KEY POINT: For a fee of 0.50%, you can buy mortgage insurance, and reduce the down payment to 5% to 10%.*

Lease with Option

As discussed in the preceding chapter, this technique has many variations. One of its purposes is to reduce your down payment or initial investment in the property.

Whether you lease or manage the property, your control over the property begins immediately—often without any down payment.

In some cases, a seller will want some money down to show good faith, but not always. After all, you are simply leasing or managing the property with the promise that at some specific date you will take title. Perhaps you won't actually take title until you have found a buyer to whom you wish to sell the property.

It's a way not only to buy control of a property now, but to defer financing it until later, when the property's increased value will make mortgage money easier to get.

■ *KEY POINT: Leasing with an option may only require a minimal down payment to secure the option.*

Management Agreement with Option

This is similar to the lease with option to buy except it usually involves a larger purchase. You wouldn't think of managing a home and then purchasing later, but you might lease it with the promise that you will take title later.

The management agreement with option might be used for an investment where the present owner doesn't want to relinquish control until he or she is satisfied with your performance. When negotiating for an apartment complex or shopping center from an institutional owner such as an insurance company from whom you'll also receive financing, the deal might be conditional on your successful handling of the job.

Properties such as apartment buildings or commercial ventures often demand your active participation. They need management from an executive perspective. In taking over this way, you'll be in a similar position as the seller. Under a strict management arrangement, being a property manager means making the decisions. The seller may not even visit the property, perhaps only meeting with you occasionally for information.

If the deal is large and complex and you want to take over but need experience and a chance to build credit, the gradual takeover of a management agreement with option to buy may be right for you. You gain control with a minimal down payment, if any at all, and acquire experience in running the enterprise (dealing with tenants, vendors, etc.) before you actually take title.

Perhaps the biggest benefit, however, is that you arrange for a purchase price in today's market but you won't have to pay it until a time in the future. This circumstance makes it easier for you to finance the deal.

■ *KEY POINT: As in leasing, a management agreement with option to buy may require only a small down payment to hold the option.*

Borrow from Relatives

A person starting out can sometimes get a little help from parents or relatives. A few thousand dollars, either as an outright gift or as a loan with a minimal interest rate, might be just enough help for a down payment.

If you don't own any property but wish to buy your first home, you'll find relatives are often willing to come to your aid. Sometimes, they got their start that way and, now that they have some money, are glad to help. Perhaps you don't need much because you can put in some yourself. You would be surprised at the number of buyers who turn to their relatives to borrow a down payment, especially for a first family home.

■ *KEY POINT: Family members will often extend a low-interest loan to help with the down payment.*

Getting a Seller to Pay Your Closing Costs

Aside from giving the mortgage itself, a seller can help you by paying the closing costs. This amount, depending on the type of loan and property, can be large.

The costs include your lawyer's fee, the title search required by the bank, transfer fees required by the Registry of Deeds, and, most costly of all, any points you might incur to start the mortgage.

You may wonder why the seller would want to pay these costs. The answer is motivation. If the seller is anxious, he or she will consider such concessions to swing the deal. If you have just enough cash for the down payment and are unable to come up with closing costs, the seller may very likely accept this burden. You could also borrow the money from the seller with a short-term note that you repay later.

In Veterans Administration financing, the seller must pay both points and any escrow fees. If eligible for a VA loan, you could buy a house with no down payment and no closing costs. However, the selling price or terms of financing may be adjusted to make up this difference. Unfortunately, sellers often boost the selling price unfairly in these situations.

■ *KEY POINT: An anxious seller may pay or loan you money for closing costs, reducing the funds needed to buy.*

Buy Out Equity on Property about to Be Foreclosed

Similar to buying a foreclosed property from a bank is buying directly from an owner whose property is being foreclosed. In

most areas, foreclosures are not common, but occasionally people default on their loans.

Sellers in financial difficulty or about to default are usually
eager to get out from under the heavy payments, even if they
must take a second mortgage for their equity. Taking over such
a loan, with no down payment, can be an excellent deal. You
could also negotiate a takeover with the bank that holds the existing loan to arrange for more money or a second mortgage,
thus freeing the seller completely.

A property owner about to default might own anything from
a single-family home to a huge apartment complex. You can
find out who's in trouble from the local banks or real estate
agents. Before foreclosing on a property, a bank must advertise
its intent in the local newspaper. That may give you several
weeks to make a deal.

Taking over a property about to be foreclosed is often done
with the bank that holds the mortgage. It offers you easy financing with hardly any down payment and relieves the seller of the
financial obligation. Lenders don't like to foreclose, so any reasonable arrangement will stop them.

■ *KEY POINT: The seller about to default is motivated to help with financing.*

Buy Foreclosed Property from the Bank

Sometimes properties are foreclosed and become the inventory
of a bank. The properties can be houses, investments, apartments, condominiums, land, or commercial blocks. They arrive
on the foreclosed list because owners, builders, or developers
have defaulted on their loans. You can take advantage of this
situation.

Most banks do not try to profit in this situation; they just want
to recoup the money they have invested in the property. You can
often get a property at less than open-market prices. If a bank
has a large amount of money invested in a property, it will often
sell to any qualified buyer for the amount of financing.

Not only will you get a discount in buying a foreclosed property, but you can take over without putting up much money. A bank might require some money down to assure your interest, but even this would be a formality.

Whether you are seeking a home or investment, talk to banks about the properties in their portfolio. You will find you can arrange a modest purchase price as well as favorable terms on a loan.

■ *KEY POINT: Once the foreclosed property is owned by the bank, you can often take over for the balance of the liability.*

Take in Partners

Americans are not used to buying property in groups, but this can be a good idea. We work together in other ways, so why not in this area?

You can buy a larger property by pooling your assets with another investor. You stretch your down payment and have more credit to sign for a larger loan.

Partnerships often work in real estate because the investment is basically a static one. Unless you're a builder, it doesn't usually require daily involvement. You're not in a store selling toasters or pork chops. You own a property that will make money for you day or night. The beauty of real estate investment is that it doesn't demand involvement except at particular times. You make money while you sleep, and this is even more true of partnerships.

Many real estate partnerships have formed over the years, small ones with a group of friends, or large, limited partnerships of 25 to 500 people sponsored by investment companies. Either way, a partnership benefits you by reducing your down payment while securing a larger property that is inherently more profitable than any you could buy alone.

■ *KEY POINT: Buying with one or more partners allows you to pool funds and take over a large property.*

THE DO'S AND DONT'S OF BUYING WITH LITTLE OR NO MONEY DOWN

The biggest problem in buying a property with little or no down payment is that its physical condition will probably be undesirable. At first, you may be attracted by favorable financing and a low purchase price. However, such properties, commonly income properties, become distressed because they have problems.

Be wary. If the property is working well—there's enough money to meet operating expenses and mortgage payments and still have some left over—there is usually no reason for the seller to accept anything less than the most attractive deal.

■ *CAUTION NOTE: When the seller will finance 100%, the property may have physical or economic problems.*

Examine the property carefully. Find out why the seller wants out. The property may need extensive repair. Physical deterioration might be causing delayed rental payments from tenants. Meeting new zoning or building code violations might be prohibitively expensive.

Arrange for a detailed report by a local building inspector.

■ *CAUTION NOTE: Inspect no-money-down property thoroughly.*

Sometimes no-money-down property is beyond saving. Unwary buyers enticed by dreams of making money in real estate have been caught in financial disasters. So put down a little money, as much down payment as you can manage, and get a better property.

■ *KEY POINT: You can often buy a more desirable property by putting down some cash.*

Another problem in lessening the down payment is handling the many mortgages simultaneously. Your monthly payments may be excessive. If it's an investment property, then you must be sure that you have enough income from the property or additional resources to meet these debts. If you buy a fully financed, single-family home to live in, your wages must be sufficient to pay the mortgage.

■ *CAUTION NOTE:* **Fully financed properties mean heavy mortgage payments.**

However, owning property is one of the fastest ways to build equity and save money for the future. If you need a home or an investment and only have a minimal down payment, this must be the way to do it. You've got to get started some time. The admonitions here give you some guidelines.

Properties whose owners are highly motivated to sell are not always a bad deal. You should just be careful; you don't want a seller's distress to become your nightmare.

■ *KEY POINT:* **Being careful in a no-money-down deal is the best way to get the right property.**

In Chapter 11, we will explore some innovative techniques for financing real estate.

INNOVATIVE TECHNIQUES FOR CREATIVE FINANCING

Although many kinds of loans have been introduced in recent years, most are simply varieties of existing loan formats.

Many experts on the consumer side of mortgage banking wonder why borrowers would select anything other than the conventional fixed-rate, 30-year mortgage. To some extent, they are right. Part of the problem is that banks hedge their bets on mortgages by promoting adjustable-rate loans. This approach protects them but doesn't always show concern for the consumer. In certain situations, however, you can find loan plans that benefit the borrower. Many of the mortgages discussed in this chapter are variations of the fixed-rate or the adjustable-rate loan with a convertible option.

■ *KEY POINT: Many loan formats are variations of fixed-rate and adjustable-rate loans.*

CONVERTING EQUITY THROUGH A REVERSE MORTGAGE

A reverse mortgage can transform a property that has real value into cash, without sale or refinancing of the property. It is actually a variant of refinancing that ends the burdensome problem of monthly payments.

■ *KEY POINT: A reverse mortgage allows you to turn equity into cash without giving up ownership.*

The amount of the loan is based on the value of the house, and the loan is either repaid at the end of a specified time, or only after the homeowner moves elsewhere or dies and the house is sold.

Many people—especially those who have lost a spouse or are contemplating retirement—don't want to leave their home and neighborhood but need some financial help. A reverse mortgage will pay them a fixed amount of money each month to cover taxes, utility costs, medical bills, and personal expenses, while deferring repayment.

Interest rates on a reverse mortgage are often variable and start at 1.625% above the rate of 1-year Treasury bills, with a 2% point annual, and a 5% lifetime cap. The financing can be done through an Individual Reverse Mortgage Account (IRMA), in which the lender receives all or part of the value of the home. This includes appreciation during the term of the loan, in return for deferring repayment until the borrower dies or decides to move. Upon the borrower's death, the estate pays off the debt.

Although there are about 2% to 3% closing costs with a typical reverse mortgage, the income you get from it depends on its size and, to a certain extent, the life expectancy of you and your spouse. If you live long, your payments from a reverse mortgage may exceed the value of the equity. If you die before equity in the property is used up, your estate must repay the lender the money you gained, with interest, plus all or a portion of the appreciation that has been gained since the mortgage was first taken out.

■ *KEY POINT: A reverse mortgage pays the borrower money in regular monthly payments.*

Again, this works well for people over the age of 60 who have property of real value they want to turn into cash. The funds from the reverse mortgage do not go to pay someone from whom you are purchasing property, but are dispersed to you at regular monthly intervals.

The danger in a reverse mortgage is that eventually the loan must be repaid or the property reverts to the full ownership and control of the lender. Most lenders require borrowers to attend counseling sessions by approved counselors before they can apply for a loan to make sure they have explored all available options. Occasionally, however, these loans make sense, particularly if a person is infirm and in need of home health care or the services of a nursing home, where large expenses are expected.

■ *CAUTION NOTE: Although a reverse mortgage converts equity to cash payments to you, it may mean final loss of ownership.*

The reverse mortgage, then, is a way in which you can convert equity in your house into regular income. Approach with caution, and only with the advice of an attorney and tax accountant.

THE PRICE-LEVEL ADJUSTED MORTGAGE (PLAM)

A PLAM is a fully amortizing loan with a long-term payoff, whose monthly payments are structured to be constant in purchasing power over the life of the loan. The initial payments on the mortgage are computed as if for a long-term, fixed-rate loan, at the prevailing real rate of interest adjusted for inflation. Sound complex? It is, but it does mean much lower monthly payments in the early years.

Here's how it works: Take an $80,000, 25-year mortgage; with a PLAM at 4.5%, the first year's monthly payments would be just under $445. With a fixed-rate mortgage at 9.5%, the monthly payments would be close to $700. Even counting in the deductibility of mortgage interest, the difference in monthly payments is considerable, making the PLAM much more affordable, particularly if you are just starting out.

■ *KEY POINT: PLAM means lower payments at the beginning of the loan.*

What PLAM does is protect the lender against inflation, because the principal amount of the mortgage based on a particular inflation rate rises accordingly. For example, at 4% inflation, the $80,000 mortgage will actually increase to $83,200 at the end of the year. In theory, this increase in debt is offset by the potential appreciation in the property. Your gamble as borrower is that the property will increase in value as fast, if not faster, than this negative amortization increases the debt. In addition, you must assume your income will increase to pay this extra amount.

■ *CAUTION NOTE: The principal balance of the PLAM loan rises along with inflation.*

It is a tradeoff: You as a borrower get lower monthly payments, and the lender's capital is protected against the unexpected higher cost of inflation. With PLAM, you do not gamble on what the future will hold. The principal is constantly adjusted to whatever the rate of inflation is. The idea is to remove the vicissitudes of inflation from the interest rate.

The advantages to a PLAM are that, to a degree, it satisfies the needs of both parties. Borrowers want low payments, and lenders want their investment back, plus interest, adjusted for what inflation took away. The outstanding balance of the loan is adjusted each month for inflation. Housing and urban development economists recommend using the urban Consumer Price Index for these adjustments.

Is this type of loan similar to the adjustable-rate mortgages that lenders have been anxious to lend out? Adjustable-rate mortgages are typically tied to short-term interest rates, such as the 1-year Treasury bill, whereas PLAMs are usually adjusted for inflation using the Consumer Price Index. The important difference between an adjustable-rate loan and a PLAM is that the underlying principal balance of a PLAM is adjusted, not the interest rate.

■ *KEY POINT: The principal balance of the loan is adjusted, not the interest rate.*

The assumption behind this arrangement is that the Consumer Price Index is going to vary less wildly than the interest rate on 1-year Treasury bills. For example, the interest rate on an adjustable-rate mortgage rising two points, say from 5% to 7%, could cause an increase in monthly payments on a 25-year, $80,000 loan from $468 a month to $565 a month. That is a sizable increase, particularly if you were struggling to meet payments before the increase. With a PLAM, in the early years of an $80,000 loan, the increase would only be $60 or $70.

One of the drawbacks of a PLAM is that you have a sense that you will never own your own home, and this is a real possibility. Large amounts of equity are pledged to the lender as time goes on in the loan. It is similar to the home equity loan, where you take a fair amount of equity and use it for other expenses. From a lender's point of view, this is an ideal way to lend money. Changes in the price level during the term of the loan are reflected not only in larger payments on the loan, but also in the outstanding balance. This gives the lender a big bonus at the end of the term.

■ *CAUTION NOTE: A PLAM may be unfairly gainful to the lender, as additional equity becomes automatically pledged as inflation rises.*

One of the biggest problems with PLAMs is finding borrowers who want to gamble on this type of financing. Although much discussed, it will take time to see if PLAMs achieve any popularity. However, if you need a mortgage with payments of $400, rather than $700 a month, you may want to investigate this option.

TWENTY-FOUR WAYS TO FINANCE A PROPERTY

Conventional Mortgages

In the conventional fixed-rate mortgage, monthly payments are set at the time you begin the loan. They are based on the overall money borrowed, the interest rate, and the number of years until the loan balance is paid off.

Interest rate and term of loan offer you flexibility. The lower the rate and amount borrowed, the lower the monthly payment. A shorter period allows you to pay the loan off more rapidly.

Interest rates vary from one source to another. The conventional fixed-rate mortgage is commonly available not only from banks, but also from alternative sources: credit unions, trust funds, and even the seller.

■ *KEY POINT: Conventional fixed-rate loans are available from many sources.*

Adjustable-Rate Mortgages (ARMs)

In this mortgage, discussed fully in Chapter 8, payments vary in amount because the interest rate varies according to a specifically chosen national indicator. Further, this may rise or fall over the life of the mortgage. An ARM is normally available only from institutional lenders.

An ARM usually starts at a slightly lower interest rate than a conventional fixed-rate mortgage. The bank wants you to borrow this way because it shifts the responsibility of shouldering the long-term effect of a rising interest rate from the bank to the borrower. The bank feels it will have greater security lending through ARMs, since the borrower must pay more if rates go up.

However, if you want to gamble that interest rates will go down from the time you borrow, an ARM might be the superior arrangement for you. You must decide if the lack of security provided by the constant payment of the fixed-rate mortgage bothers you. It is a little like horse racing. If you feel the lower interest rate will win, that is the one to bet on.

■ *KEY POINT:* *The interest rate in an ARM varies according to a national economic indicator.*

Second and Third Mortgages

A common way for a seller to help a buyer is to offer a second mortgage. It's the oldest form of creative financing. This money is borrowed over the amount of the first mortgage; for example, you borrow 80% of the property's selling price from a bank. The seller, being motivated, gives you another 10% to 15% as a loan. Often the holding period for a second mortgage is shorter than the terms you might get with a conventional or adjustable-rate loan, perhaps 5 to 10 years compared with 20 or 30 years.

■ *KEY POINT:* *A second mortgage is a fixed-rate loan over the first mortgage.*

Second mortgages are common in financing investment property. Here, a buyer often assumes an existing mortgage that might be low compared with the current selling price. For example, in assuming a loan of 50% of value, most buyers don't have or aren't willing to put up another 50% as a down payment. To make the deal, it is not unreasonable for the seller to offer another 40% as a second mortgage. The terms and interest rate may be similar to what a bank would charge for new money. However, it allows you to purchase at a nominal 10% cash. And you have the benefit of the assumed loan with its lower rate.

■ *KEY POINT:* *Second mortgages are usually given by the seller to reduce the buyer's down payment.*

Only under special circumstances should a second or third mortgage be negotiated with a quick payoff. Having to pay off a large sum within a year or two might strap you financially. It can work, however, if you are expecting some cash, such as an inheritance, to come your way when the amount is due. For example, let's say you buy a home and the seller furnishes the first $5,000 of the purchase price without any repayment required from you until the following year. While that may be fine to get you into the house, it may endanger your chances of keeping the property if you are forced to come up with a lump-sum payment that could be beyond your means.

■ *CAUTION NOTE: Plan for additional funds when second mortgages have quick payoffs.*

Normally, structure a second or third mortgage like a conventional loan with a fixed interest rate and monthly, quarterly, or semiannual payments that can be made out of your income or cash from your investment.

Seller Financing

Seller financing is the easiest way to create instant money. In effect, the seller loans you equity he or she already has in the property and receives that equity back in the form of payments based on a negotiated interest rate over time until the full amount of this equity is paid off.

■ *KEY POINT: Seller financing means a purchase is made with part or all the mortgage funds coming from the seller's equity.*

Seller financing is similar to a bank giving you a first mortgage (80%–90% of the property's value as a loan), but instead you receive it from the seller.

■ *KEY POINT: Most seller financing is in the form of conventional fixed-rate loans.*

There are many ways to devise seller financing, often called "creative financing." More ways are explained in Chapter 9. When buying any property, you should always consider having the seller give you back a mortgage at terms more helpful than you could get from an institutional source.

■ *KEY POINT: In buying property, always consider asking the seller for financing.*

Purchase Money Mortgages

A purchase money mortgage is a mortgage financed by the seller. It is the most common way for a seller to help a buyer. These mortgages are usually fixed-rate loans with constant payments.

In a purchase money mortgage, a portion, if not all, of the money used to purchase the property is in the form of a mortgage held by the seller. It might be a first, second, or third mortgage.

■ *KEY POINT: Purchase money mortgages are mortgages given by the seller.*

Assumed Mortgages

A loan that is transferred from a seller to a buyer is called a mortgage assumption. The buyer assumes the obligation to pay the old mortgage based on its interest rate and remaining term.

Since the balance of the assumed mortgage has been reduced by payments over time, it is low in relation to the current selling price. Additional financing is usually necessary when you assume a loan.

■ *KEY POINT: Assuming a mortgage means taking over a seller's loan balance.*

The purpose of assuming a mortgage is to take over a low-interest loan. Banks don't like you to assume one of their loans. For years, they have stipulated in their agreements that a second borrower cannot take over a loan. However, if this clause is not in the agreement (consult your lawyer), you may save yourself a considerable amount of cash.

Some court decisions have stated that banks must allow these takeovers. A bank may allow one if it can pass a favorable judgment on the borrower's creditworthiness. In giving you permission to take over, the bank sometimes even releases the previous borrower from liability on the loan.

■ *CAUTION NOTE:*   *Many loans are not assumable.*

Assuming the mortgage means taking the mortgage "subject to" loan; you're simply taking over the loan payment without negotiation with the original mortgage lender. You need to discuss the prevailing banking practices in your area with your lawyer or real estate agent to determine what laws may affect the assumption of the mortgage.

When possible, it is an excellent way to finance. As shown in Chapter 1, the balance on recent loans does not decrease until the later stages of the loan and can thus take many years. Still, in the first 5 or 10 years of an assumed mortgage, a fair amount of principal can be paid off.

Government-Backed Loans

Government FHA Loans.   Federal Housing Administration loans vary in availability and the amount of money a person can borrow from time to time. Different programs are sponsored by the FHA. Some programs give money directly; others guarantee to a local lender the repayment of the money. Most guarantee a lower interest rate. This benefit is sometimes lessened because the lender charges points to originate the loan. A good bit of paperwork slows down the purchase process. The FHA is not the place to get a quick commitment.

■ *KEY POINT:*   *Although FHA loan commitments are slow, they allow low down payments.*

Government VA Guarantee.   A government Veterans Administration guarantee is similar to the FHA loan, but you must be a veteran. Called the GI loan, it also limits the amount you can finance. The loans are given for homes only. The FHA insists on a minimal down payment; the VA loan can require no down payment unless the loan amount is over a particular limit. Again, the institutional lender can charge points and can manipulate the terms and conditions of the loan.

Consider this route if you are a veteran and buying your first home.

■ *KEY POINT: If you are a veteran, you can apply for a GI loan with little or no down payment.*

FmHA Mortgages.   Loans from the Farmers Home Administration should be considered by low- and moderate-income borrowers from rural areas with base populations of less than 10,000. It provides loans for single-family homes. And you do not need to be a farmer. The main program known as "502" home loan, has a budget of about $1.2 billion. Its guaranteed loan program has a budget of about $400 million.

The unique feature is that, if you qualify under its low-income ceiling, you can put zero money down and pay as little as 1% interest, depending on family income. To qualify, your adjusted gross income (gross income minus child-care costs and $480 per child) must fall below 80% of your county's median income. For example, a family of four making $28,000 or less in adjusted income is likely to qualify. However, FmHA is the lender of last resort. You must be unable to get a loan from another source. Your monthly payment of interest and principal, including taxes and insurance, is set at 20% of adjusted income. The program subsidizes the rest of the payment, effectively reducing the loan's interest rate to as low as 1%.

■ *KEY POINT: FmHA provides direct low-cost loans for those who qualify.*

FmHA reviews these terms every 12 months. The required payment can rise or fall according to your income. All that's required is a good job and good credit. One hitch can snag superb plans: Once your income reaches a level sufficient to receive a mortgage from a local lender, the Feds require that you refinance.

Once the house is sold, the FmHA requires that a percentage of appreciation be used to pay back the subsidy. This is at no interest. Further, if there was no appreciation, you pay nothing.

■ *CAUTION NOTE: FmHA requires part of appreciation to pay back its subsidy.*

So, for a loan that requires no down payment, no title insurance, no loan origination fee, no escrow, and only modest other closing costs, contact the FmHA.

FmHA Loan Guarantees. The Guaranteed Rural Housing Loan Program is similar to the loans backed by the FHA and VA. The loans are made by private lenders with 90% of the principal guaranteed by the FmHA.

As with the direct FmHA loans, these guarantees are available only in rural areas. Other details include a maximum mortgage amount (same as FHA) of $67,500 for most rural counties. No down payment is required. Income must be less than 115% of the county's median income. A 1% origination fee to the lender is typical. Further, a fee is charged by FmHA of 0.9% of the loan amount. Two months' escrow for taxes and insurance must be established.

■ *KEY POINT: For qualified borrowers, FmHA provides the local lender with a loan guarantee.*

Lease with Option to Buy

Any time you're short of cash for a down payment, you can lease a property with an option to buy it at a later time. This gives you a way to take over use of the property without the full cost of ownership. You don't even have to talk to the bank. Financing will come later when you exercise your option.

Rarely do you have to make a full down payment to take over. Often, only 1% to 5% of the agreed-on price will suffice for the option.

The lease with option gives you time to investigate the property before buying. Often used by professional investors, it is a readily adaptable device to take over a parcel of land on which you might wish to build or a house on which the seller is willing to defer the closing.

This method is thoroughly explained in Chapter 9.

■ *KEY POINT: The lease with option to buy allows you to control the property while deferring the purchase decision.*

Management Agreement with Option to Buy

Here's another way to take over a property while deferring purchase and financing. It is an easy way to take control with no down payment except for any monies advanced to secure the option with the seller.

This agreement is the same as the lease with option to buy except that your control over the property is greater. You are the manager, taking the place of the seller. If, for example, the property is a commercial building with tenants, they must report and pay their rent to you. In turn, you accept the responsibilities of the owner in dealing with their needs.

The management agreement with option to buy, like the lease with option to buy, allows time in which to become familiar with the property before purchasing. There is more information on this unique way of taking control of a property in Chapter 9.

■ *KEY POINT: The management agreement with option to buy puts you in the position of ownership before actually purchasing.*

Sale-Leaseback

Some investors shop for opportunities to take over a property in a sale-leaseback. These deals usually involve an established single tenant, such as a fast-food chain or an automobile dealership.

Often, a business that has owned and occupied a commercial property for some years, having depreciated it for tax purposes, finds it beneficial to sell the building, get the cash for it, and remain as a tenant. It is an easy deal for you to negotiate, and you end up with the property and a tenant who is the former owner.

■ *KEY POINT: A sale-leaseback is usually a property bought from a seller who remains as a tenant.*

In some cases, the seller may give you a mortgage that fully finances the purchase. Often you can buy this way with a minimal down payment.

■ *KEY POINT: A sale-leaseback is often financed by the seller.*

You then have an investment in which all mortgage costs are paid for by the rent. You are also able to take the building (not the land) portion of the property based on the current sale price and make depreciation deductions.

Why does the original owner want to do this? Simple: to get a lot of cash from you in the form of a mortgage plus any down payment that you might provide. The owner can now use this cash to buy equipment to make more hamburgers or widgets. And, almost as important, the former owner, who had used up all depreciable (taxable) assets, can now deduct the rent payments.

A sale-leaseback is an excellent arrangement to make as a joint venture or partnership with other investors. As with any purchasing or financing arrangement, a knowledgeable attorney with a specialty in taxes should structure the investment.

■ *KEY POINT: Sale-leasebacks usually involve other investors.*

Trade-in Property or Chattel Goods

One way to reduce the need for a down payment is for a willing seller to take payment in other value than cash. An automobile, boat, stocks or bonds, or even other real estate, such as a vacation home or parcel of land, could be accepted by the seller as part of the deal.

Stocks and bonds have a specific value easily verified by a seller. This saves you the burden of selling the stock and paying taxes on the transaction.

More often than you think, a seller of a home or investment property will accept a car or even a boat. It may seem odd, but any sale reflects the seller's level of motivation. If it's strong enough, that seller is likely to accept chattel goods. Sometimes, in a strong desire to change and move on, sellers just want out.

■ *KEY POINT: Down payments can often be tangible goods such as cars or boats, or anything the seller might accept.*

Exchanging Property

Exchanging property means trading one property for another. Usually, the trading of one investment property for another is known as a "like-kind" exchange.

By transferring the tax result into the second property, you can defer the tax on your profit until you sell this second property. Investors who specialize in exchanging move their profits through several trades before they pay a tax.

Exchanging is considered one of the fastest ways to build equity in real estate (see Chapter 9).

■ *KEY POINT: Immense fortunes can be made in trading one property for another.*

The Wraparound Mortgage

The wraparound mortgage, or all-inclusive mortgage, encompasses all the existing first, second, and third mortgages plus any new money loaned by a lender. The mortgage then "wraps around" the existing mortgages.

The wraparound is an excellent technique when the existing mortgages have a low interest rate and are unassumable (see Chapter 9).

■ *KEY POINT: The wraparound allows you to take over existing financing by making an overall mortgage with the seller.*

Commercial or Personal Loans

You don't always have to negotiate formal mortgages at a bank to borrow the money needed to purchase. With a purchase money mortgage from the seller, a personal or business loan from a commercial bank can make up the down payment.

Banks that lend money in the form of personal loans aren't as fussy as in the past about the purpose of the loan. Often, that extra $5,000 or $10,000 needed to make a deal can be gotten with just your signature—without all the appraisals or signing of papers.

■ *KEY POINT: A commercial or personal loan can be used as a down payment.*

Usually, you must have previously established good credit to get a personal loan. Some establish credit by borrowing money, putting it in a savings account, and then paying it back when it is due. Often, the only security for the bank is your good faith in making payments.

In some areas, you don't need as exemplary a credit history for getting a $70,000 mortgage on a house or commercial property as you do in borrowing $5,000 in the form of a personal loan. This happens, in part, because the property itself is the security for the mortgage, while your ability to pay is the only security for the personal loan.

Limited Partnership

A limited partnership consists of a group of investors who pool their money for investment. A general partner controls the enterprise. A commercial or residential development, whether an existing or a new property, could be the investment.

A limited partnership benefits you, as a limited partner, because you become part owner of a property larger than you could purchase on your own. Also, you don't participate directly in the arrangement for the mortgage; a general partner negotiates the financing.

■ *KEY POINT: Combining your funds with other investors' funds in a limited partnership allows purchase of a larger investment.*

Whether the group involves 6 or 600 people, you will "own" a respective amount of equity in proportion to the total equity of the property. This includes a proportionate share of the property's mortgage. For example, if you invest $10,000 along with 9 other investors, you have $100,000. With that down payment, you can buy a $500,000 property, $400,000 of which if financed, perhaps by a large mortgage bank or an insurance company.

You put $10,000 of equity into the property plus a "share" of the mortgage of $40,000. You didn't have to go out and negotiate or commit yourself personally for this mortgage. The net effect of your $10,000 is that it buys a $50,000 deal, as if you bought a house for $50,000 and put $10,000 down.

A limited partnership is an excellent way to purchase a larger investment than you would normally negotiate on your own while remaining free of the property's management. The general partner runs the partnership. As many investors have found out, however, these investments are only as strong as the property the partnership controls. Too high an original purchase price, exorbitant brokerage fees, or unreasonable commissions for the continued management of the project have soured some investments. However, if you enter into an agreement wisely, with full knowledge of the property, the aims of the group of investors, and the general partner, limited partnerships can be an excellent way to finance and own property.

■ *CAUTION NOTE: A limited partnership is only as good as the property it buys.*

Life Estate

An unusual way to purchase with unique benefits for both the buyer and seller is commonly known as the life estate purchase. Although this type of transaction has different forms, normally a seller becomes a tenant in his or her own house. For example, a seller, perhaps an older woman lacking dependents or an adequate income to sustain her over the remaining years of her life, sells her property to an investor but remains a tenant. She gives a mortgage, accepting a minimal down payment. She will receive monthly payments based on an annuity for the remainder of her life.

In effect, the seller has her house, continues to live in it, and receives an income without the burden of rent or property taxes. The investor gambles that the value of the property will grow.

■ *KEY POINT: In a life estate purchase, a seller who gives the mortgage remains as a tenant for life.*

What is your source of money to give the seller each month for property you don't have use of and cannot rent out? This arrangement is commonly negotiated so payments to the seller are based on an annuity factored by the projected remaining years of that person's life. For example, if you as the investor, gamble that this person will live 10 more years, you will expect to pay monthly payments for that 10-year period. Factored into these payments is a reasonable interest rate based on the 10-year term.

This may not be like a mortgage, but computations of the monthly payments are similar. You, as the investor, own the property. To make it work financially for you, mortgage the property with a bank, reinvest this money in a safe, insured manner, and, in turn, make payments to the bank and to the seller.

As you can see, the life estate method has advantages for both buyer and seller. The seller gets a lifetime annuity for a property based on today's value.

Tomorrow's value to the seller is unimportant, since no one can spend money after they're dead. And if the seller outlives the original projection of his or her remaining years (the payments having been based on such figures from an annuity table), he or she can thereby receive more money than expected from the original "mortgage." In addition to this income, the seller retains possession of his or her home.

The advantage for you as an investor is that you don't have to put down much money to gain the property. The property will increase in value with little effort on your part. However, you must be cautious. The stream of money needed to make payments to the seller, now your tenant, can be difficult to find. And, as discussed, the seller may live longer than anticipated, holding up final possession of the property. However, if you can arrive at a satisfactory payment plan, this arrangement can provide a big bonus for you in the future.

■ *CAUTION NOTE: Sellers can remain as life tenants for a long time.*

Refinance on Purchase

The refinance on purchase involves taking possession of a property and then refinancing the property for more than the original loans you assumed or placed. You do this to gain back some of the equity or cash down payment you placed on it. It can be done to get out from under a short-term second mortgage, meet a large payment deadline, or simply put some cash in your pocket.

A typical way to use this technique is to wait some minimal time, perhaps a year after purchase, until you have made improvements and the property has increased in value. Often, a bank is willing to increase its commitment on the mortgage. These are not difficult loans to get if the bank is convinced there has been a change in value and the total amount of the mortgage does not appear excessive.

■ *KEY POINT: Refinance on purchase is asking the bank for more money after you take title.*

Borrow on Equity

Borrowing on equity is similar to the refinance on purchase except that you have a large amount of equity that you may wish to either put in your pocket or use as security for another mortgage.

Both savings banks and commercial banks can be approached to refinance your equity. Such loans don't always have to be secured by an official mortgage instrument, as you could receive the equity in the form of a personal loan. Or, a commercial bank, even a savings bank, can negotiate second mortgages beyond an existing first, thus releasing equity money to you.

■ *KEY POINT: Once you have equity, you can refinance.*

Blanket Mortgage

This mortgage covers more than one property. It is ideal when you buy a second home, for example, a vacation home. You put up your present home, or other property, as security for the new property.

You may think, "Well, why isn't the second home a security in itself?" True, you wouldn't have to merge the two properties in one mortgage in most cases. commonly, though, the second or vacation home is in another area, perhaps another state, and banks get worried about lending money for properties in unfamiliar locations. The equity in your present home serves as security for what becomes an overall blanket loan on both properties. It can often make the deal, especially when you are buying in another area.

■ *KEY POINT: In a blanket mortgage, your present property acts as security for an overall loan covering a new, additional property.*

Contract for Deed

The contract for deed, or land sales contract, has varying names in different areas of the country. This is another technique used when it is impossible to take over existing financing or when no financing exists at all, and you wish to make only a small down payment. Here the seller retains legal title to the property.

In a contract for deed, the seller gives you a large balance in the form of a mortgage but retains title to the property until the mortgage or "contract" is paid off. The deed is usually held in escrow and recorded only upon the final payoff.

■ *KEY POINT: In the contract for deed, the seller gives the financing and holds the deed in escrow until the mortgage is paid off.*

This type of purchase is similar to the management agreement with option to buy in that it is issued when present financing is difficult. However, it is used by the homeowner instead of an investor.

The seller benefits by making the sale when money is tight and interest rates are high. You benefit by purchasing at a negotiated, lower interest rate and down payment. The seller feels secure in the sale since he or she still holds legal title to the property in case of default.

A contract for deed, or land sales contract, was more popular in the past and is not used as much today. However, it is still a valid device for buying a property when financing is difficult.

■ *KEY POINT: The contract for deed technique is used when new financing is scarce.*

Trust Deeds

In using a trust deed to purchase, you get a mortgage from the seller after a nominal down payment. The seller then signs the deed, held in trust until the mortgage has been fully paid.

Similar to the contract for deed, it is used when the seller must finance because of a lack of existing mortgage money.

■ *KEY POINT: In a trust deed, the seller gives the mortgage and holds the deed until it is paid off.*

Trust Deed with Balloon Payment

The trust deed with balloon payment is similar to the trust deed except that at a specific time a large payment is made on the mortgage, either reducing it substantially or paying it off entirely. Now, the deed is released from escrow and given to you for recording.

The trust deed with balloon payment encourages a seller to give financing, as he or she will be paid off (in a shorter amount of time than under other agreements) when the mortgage balloons.

■ *KEY POINT: The trust deed with balloon payment can convince a seller to finance for a short time.*

■ *CAUTION NOTE: Future funds must be earmarked to meet balloon provisions in mortgages.*

Repurchase Option

The repurchase option is a way to sell a property that you own while retaining the right to repurchase it at some future time. It is a guarantee that you can regain the use of an asset you don't currently need.

■ *KEY POINT: The repurchase option allows you to sell now and rebuy later.*

The repurchase option is normally used for business property, for example, when the use of a particular building is changed for a short time.

Also, when used with other mortgages, it allows you to sell at a lower-than-market value and interest rate, and receive a large amount of cash that can temporarily be used for other purposes. Further, you can repurchase the same property later at a predetermined price. In exercising your option to rebuy, you could then sell it at a higher price.

The Biweekly Mortgage

The biweekly mortgage is an opportunity for you to shorten the term of your loan and reduce the interest costs a slight amount each month. It works this way: You pay half the monthly payment on a fixed-rate mortgage every two weeks; that is, 26 payments a year to make the 13 monthly installments. The results can be dramatic: A 30-year mortgage can often be paid off in little more than 20 years, saving large amounts, perhaps thousands of dollars, in interest.

■ *KEY POINT: Making biweekly payments dramatically lowers interest paid.*

Often, slightly lower interest rates are available for biweekly loans, since payments must be made twice as often. An automatic payment plan, such as a money market account, from which the bank extracts the payment directly, is advisable. For many people who are paid every other week, the biweekly mortgage can be a little bit more convenient.

■ *KEY POINT: The interest rate for a biweekly mortgage is often less because of the lender's faster recapture of capital.*

In a biweekly mortgage, each payment is half of what you would normally give to the bank each month under a conventional mortgage, but you pay it twice a month. Except for February, all months are a few days longer than four weeks, so you actually make 26 payments a year, not 24—an extra month's installment. Let's compare a $100,000 loan with monthly payments at an interest rate of 9% and a term of 30 years with the same loan paid biweekly. At 9%, your biweekly payments would be $402 and you wind up paying $804 more a year than if you paid monthly. However, you would be paying almost $60,420 less in interest, plus you would retire your mortgage in about 22 years (570 two-week periods) rather than 30—a real saving for those who can organize themselves and who have the extra income to pay the mortgage every other week.

These are only a few of the many ways in which you can finance real estate. They provide proof that unique arrangements are possible when the motivations of buyers and sellers are strong.

In the following chapters, we will discuss more of these techniques. You will see how you can use them to your advantage and how you can make complex arrangements to gain satisfactory financing in the quickest possible time.

In Chapter 12, you will learn how to free up equity in your present home.

HOME EQUITY LOANS 12

Home equity loans are a speedy way to raise cash. Instead of refinancing your mortgage or negotiating a second mortgage, consider what is basically a readily accessible line of credit backed up by the equity in your home.

■ *KEY POINT: A home equity loan is a line of credit backed up by the equity in your home.*

As you have seen, mortgage interest is still deductible under the latest tax code. This makes it one of the only ways in which to borrow money with tax-free interest.

CASH IN YOUR HOME SECURED BY A MORTGAGE

An equity loan or equity credit line is credit secured by a mortgage on your home. It is a variation of the second mortgage. The unmortgaged value or equity of your home is turned into a revolving line of credit that can be easily tapped by a check or credit card.

A home equity loan is usually priced at a modest two percentage points above the prime rate; therefore it is an attractive means of raising extra cash. Conventional second mortgages can often run three to four percentage points higher than first mortgages.

■ *KEY POINT: A home equity loan is an attractive alternative to a higher priced second mortgage.*

One of the problems with a variable-rate equity loan is that the interest rate is not fixed but usually based on the movable prime rate. This allows it to float upward and downward, which can often mean a higher rate in an uncertain future. Further, like a second mortgage, this loan is secured by a lien on your home. And, you do run the risk of losing your property if you get in over your head and can't pay. You must approach the home equity loan with caution, but if you need some cash, it is an option to explore.

■ *CAUTION NOTE: Interest rates can escalate in the future.*

■ *CAUTION NOTE: Use caution, as difficulty in paying can mean the possible loss of your home.*

MAJOR TYPES OF HOME EQUITY LOAN

The first type of home equity loan is one in which the money is borrowed and paid back over a specific period with a fixed or floating interest rate.

Choosing between a fixed or floating interest rate depends on what the rates are when you start the loan. It is similar to choosing between conventional and adjustable-rate mortgages—it may be better to pay the fixed rate, although a little higher, because you know that the interest is not going to change.

Another type of home equity loan is the equity line of credit. Here you need not take the total amount you negotiate for at one time but draw on it as you need it. This way, you pay interest only on the amount you use. The disadvantage is that you pay the closing charges on setting up the credit line whether you use the money or not. Generally, you repay this type of loan in monthly installments that pay interest on the money you've taken and the reduced principal. Interest rates can be either fixed or floating, and although you may wish to negotiate a helpful fixed rate, most banks only offer this type of loan with a floating rate.

■ *CAUTION NOTE: Closing costs are the same regardless of the amount drawn.*

■ *KEY POINT: A floating interest rate is the most common in an equity line of credit.*

COMPARING BASIC ELEMENTS

Home equity loans were invented in the mid-1980s, and most banks now offer them. Let's look at some of the basic elements of a home equity loan, so when you talk to various banks about this opportunity, you can make the following comparisons.

How Will the Rate of Interest Change?

The interest rate for a home equity loan is usually not fixed. In this way, it is similar to the interest rate on an adjustable-rate mortgage. Most banks use the prime rate as an index, adding on the average two percentage points to set the beginning rate for the borrower. Usually this rate is adjusted monthly, but some banks adjust it quarterly.

■ *KEY POINT: The prime rate plus two points is a commonly used index for home equity loan interest.*

The bank will want to set some parameters for the loan. A particular point for you to be cautious about is the base interest rate—the minimum rate the bank will want to charge. The problem is that if your rate is set at two percentage points over the prime rate but the bank has set a 9.5% base rate, you could still be paying 9.5% even when the prime rate is 6%.

■ *CAUTION NOTE: A high base rate stops the loan interest from drifting lower.*

Again, as with adjustable-rate mortgages, beware of a low promotional rate that makes the loan look like a good deal. For example, a lender might charge 4% for the first two months of your loan and then convert to the prime plus two percentage points. If you want a deal like this, make sure the six-month period starts when your loan closes and not on the date of application.

■ *CAUTION NOTE: A low promotional rate can escalate rapidly.*

Second, make sure that you can afford the higher payment six months later. If you can barely squeak by paying the lower, introductory interest rate, you may not be able to meet the payments when the rate jumps up three or four points.

■ *CAUTION NOTE: When the rate rises, larger payments can cause difficulty.*

The variable-rate loans usually have some sort of cap on the interest rate over a set period of years, such as five years or over the life of the loan. That's not the way most banks want to negotiate their home equity loans with you. However, competition among banks is forcing them to come up with some new techniques, such as letting you lock in an interest rate cap at origination or some future time. They even allow a conversion to a conventional loan, which might be proper when you have solved your immediate short-term cash needs.

■ *KEY POINT: Conversion to a conventional loan may be possible.*

How Much Money Can You Borrow?

As with most conventional loans, mortgage lenders will lend or extend a line of credit up to 70% or 80% of your home's unencumbered equity. This means that if you have a home valued at $200,000 but already have a balance on a first mortgage of $75,000, the bank is not going to lend you 80% of the $200,000 but up to 80% of the remaining equity of $125,000. Your line of credit is thus $100,000.

■ *KEY POINT:*   *The maximum loan is 80% of equity only.*

For homes valued more than $250,000, most banks tighten the rules somewhat, allowing perhaps only 75% instead of 80% of unencumbered equity as a line of credit. Again, this is a matter of negotiation; often, it is helpful to go to the bank that holds your present mortgage to negotiate a home equity loan. If you have a good payment record that assures the bank you can make these higher payments, they will look favorably on your request for the highest credit line possible.

■ *KEY POINT:*   *A consistent record of payments is helpful in securing an equity loan from your current mortgage holder.*

The question of how much money you wish to borrow under the equity line of credit may be based on how much of the amount will be deductible.

How Do Closing Costs Vary?

When you got your first mortgage for your home, whether it was a conventional or an adjustable-rate loan, your closing costs probably averaged between 4% and 5% of the amount of money you were borrowing. An equity line of credit also involves some closing costs. Generally, they will not be quite as much but will range from about 1% to 2% or 3%, depending on your area.

■ *KEY POINT:*   *Closing costs for a home equity loan are usually half of those for a first mortgage.*

These closing costs can be extensive, however, and you must remember that you are not borrowing all the money you are signing up for at the time of closing. The loan is a line of credit;

you are going to take it out as you need it, but you must pay the closing costs up front based on the whole amount of the credit line. If you are taking out an equity line of credit of $80,000 and your fee is $1,150, that is 1.4% of the loan amount. It sounds reasonable, but if you only use $30,000, the closing cost of $1,150 is 3.8%. Thus, you may pay excessive closing costs unless you are going to receive in the short term the largest portion of the amount of the loan you negotiate.

■ *CAUTION NOTE:* *Closing costs are based on the potential amount that can be borrowed.*

What is included in the loan fees? The service fee for the bank, legal fees, and a new title insurance policy (this will not always be required if you are negotiating with the same bank). As with your first mortgage, an appraisal, perhaps documentary tax stamps, and recording fees also need to be paid. You can charge these closing costs off as your first draw rather than come up with extra cash.

Schedule of Repayment

Your monthly payment of interest and principal is usually calculated as a percentage of the combined principal and interest outstanding, with the interest repaid first at the end of each billing period. If there is any amount that remains to be paid at the end of this term, it is usually covered with a balloon payment.

You must remember that with an equity credit line loan you are only drawing off money as you need it. Your payments may not be high until you start borrowing a large amount of money. A 1% to 2% minimum monthly interest rate is common. Note that 2% over the period of a year is 24%. You want to make sure that you are reducing as much principal as possible, thereby negotiating the lowest possible interest rate.

■ *KEY POINT:* *A lower amount of initial borrowing is reflected in lower payments.*

Some banks allow repayment of interest monthly, withholding the payment on any principal until the end of the loan as a balloon payment. This is helpful. For example, if because of your job or personal requirements you must sell your home, perhaps at the end of five years, you can sell and pay off the amount of money you borrowed through the credit line.

■ *KEY POINT: Paying interest first works well if you will be selling soon.*

In either of these cases, should any additional payment of principal be made, banks usually will not charge a penalty. It is an opportunity for you if you receive an inheritance or other large gain before the end of the mortgage term.

Deductibility of Home Equity Loans

Since equity line of credit loans were introduced, the rules for interest deductibility have changed. Now all interest on home equity loans up to $100,000 is deductible (note exception for wealthy individuals described later in this chapter). This is much simpler than the previous deductibility, limited to the amount borrowed up to the purchase price of your home and the costs of any improvements.

■ *KEY POINT: Interest is deductible up to $100,000.*

Before, only interest on loans for financing, medical treatment, and educational expenses such as tuition and fees for you or your family was deductible. This method was difficult to calculate, as you had to determine the average unpaid balance of your mortgage for the year in question. So, the new home equity loan rule is a genuine tax boon, allowing you to deduct interest on the loan up to $100,000 ($50,000 if you are married and filing separately).

However, regardless of how you use the money, the loan cannot exceed your house or second home's fair market value. Beyond $100,000, while the funds are still borrowed against equity on your home, the amount of interest deducted will depend on the way any excess money is spent. If you use it for business purposes, it is fully deductible, but if you use it for investment purposes, you can deduct only up to the amount of investment income plus $4,000. If you use the money for another purpose, it is treated as a consumer loan with no deductibility.

■ *KEY POINT: Interest is fully deductible on home equity funds exceeding $100,000 if used in business.*

■ *CAUTION NOTE: Interest on funds exceeding $100,000 used for investment purposes is deductible only to the extent of the investment income plus $4,000.*

Who benefits? Under previous rules there was no limit to the deductibility if the money went to educational or medical expenses for you or your dependents. Now, with the limit at $100,000, you can do anything with that money without infringing on its deductibility; beyond $100,000, it is deductible only if used for business. If you have several children attending college at the same time and your tuition expenses are high, the home equity loan can benefit you as long as you don't go over $100,000. You can particularly benefit from getting a home equity loan if you bought your house years ago when real estate prices were low. There is plenty of equity in your property now against which the bank can extend you a line of credit.

■ *CAUTION NOTE: Interest on home equity funds in excess of $100,000 is not deductible even if the loan is for college tuition.*

The money from a home equity loan is not usually used to acquire property or improve a residence. It is more often used to meet outside financial obligations such as college tuition.

Proceeds of the loan are fully deductible as long as the debt does not exceed the lesser of fair market value of your home, minus the existing mortgage balance, or $100,000 ($50,000 if married and filing separate returns). Even if you own two homes as primary and secondary residences, the tax cap on your home equity debt cannot exceed $100,000.

Keep in mind this $100,000 ceiling on a home equity loan. If you are just purchasing your first home and don't need the money right away, increase the mortgage used to purchase your home. In this way, you can save the money you'll need later. When you want to get your home equity loan, you don't eat into your $100,000 equity ceiling.

■ *CAUTION NOTE: The deductibility ceiling for the proceeds of a home equity loan is $100,000.*

An important note on deductibility: Always check with your accountant to make sure that the interest is indeed deductible. If you are a prosperous individual subject to the Alternative Minimum Tax, or AMT, interest on up to $100,000 of home equity debt is deductible only if the money is used to purchase or improve your first or second home.

■ *CAUTION NOTE: Always check with accountant to verify deductibility of home equity loan interest.*

KEEP BOOKKEEPING IN ORDER

You may benefit by depositing your borrowed money in its own checking account. The Internal Revenue Service has been known to disallow deductions for people who fail to keep track of where their borrowed funds go.

■ *CAUTION NOTE: The IRS may disallow deductions not backed up by accurate bookkeeping.*

If you keep your home equity loan proceeds in the same account as your regular income or investment dividends, how you spent the money can become unclear. Keep the funds in a separate account, particularly if the money you are going to be spending is more than $100,000. Anything less than $100,000, since it is deductible however you spend it, does not need a special account or even accurate records.

It is not hard to keep track of what is and is not deductible. You will get a monthly statement from your lender showing you the interest that is eligible for a tax deduction if you borrowed under $100,000. If you borrowed more than that, careful records will protect you if you are audited, since you will have to protect anything you deducted beyond the $100,000 from being treated as consumer interest.

■ *KEY POINT: For home equity borrowing beyond $100,000, consider a separate account to keep track of expenses.*

THREE QUESTIONS YOU NEED TO ASK YOURSELF ABOUT APPLYING FOR A HOME EQUITY LOAN

First, is it in your interest to get funds through the equity credit line? Second, is your interest deductibility endangered by the type of investment you make with the money? Third, how constrained are you in spending the money to get the maximum tax benefits?

As with any loan, wise use of the funds is gained without spending cash. The advantage of the credit line is that you do not need to borrow the actual money until you need it. It is a line of credit secured by the equity in your home.

All interest on loans less than $100,000 is deductible no matter how you spend the money. After $100,000, the excess money is deductible only if used in your business or investment up to the amount of your investment income plus $4,000. Otherwise, it is regarded as a consumer loan.

■ *KEY POINT: Don't draw money or pay interest until it is needed.*

If you manage the funds from a home equity loan carefully, it can be a low-cost way to finance necessary major expenses. The interest rates, although higher than conventional loans, are less than credit card loans of 15% to 20%. And as long as you don't need to borrow more than $100,000, all the interest is deductible.

■ *KEY POINT: Interest on home equity loans costs less than that on many other borrowing methods.*

If you borrow more, you can still write off the interest in full if you use the money in your business or if the amount is equal to your investment income plus $4,000.

PROBLEMS WITH BORROWING HOME EQUITY MONEY

A word of caution is in order. Any time you use your existing house as collateral for a loan, you can lose it if you fail to make your payments. In times of varying interest rates, the monthly payment on a home equity loan could rise strongly.

Equally dangerous is a loan that charges interest only, requiring you to pay back the balance of the loan in a single sum at some future time. This would cause you either to sell your home to pay off the loan or take out another loan at a much higher interest rate. So, beware of initial low monthly payments that cover only the interest. You will be liable for a balloon payment at the end of the loan period representing the principal you borrowed but have not yet repaid.

■ *CAUTION NOTE: A potential rise in rate, hence payments, and a balloon payoff can endanger home ownership.*

One of the significant problems with home equity loans is that they draw down value in your home. Ten years ago, homeowners controlled over two-thirds of the equity in their homes. Owing to falling values and increased borrowing, today that ownership is closer to one-half.

The solution is to borrow only what you can afford. The decision to borrow should never be frivolous. If you load yourself up with debt, you endanger the continued ownership of your home. Needed home improvements, education, and medical care may be required expenses. Cars, boats, and other big-ticket items are not, plus they depreciate far more rapidly than a home. Wise financial planners would question the decision to spend tax-deductible money on something that's losing value. Remember, any tax savings is usually exceeded by the higher interest cost of the home equity loan.

■ *CAUTION NOTE: Large debt payments can endanger home ownership.*

Banks benefit by lending out their money through a home equity program. Their interest rate, averaging two percentage points over prime, guarantees them a profit no matter how the financial markets may vary. To you, these loans can be a real danger if the interest rates climb or if your income declines.

So beware. If rates climb, and they surely will from current lows, repayment can drag on for many years. The situation is made more difficult because many banks advertise a low rate to get you started and, three to six months later, convert that rate to a much higher one.

Look for a bank that will give you a cap on the interest rate, and avoid a repayment plan that doesn't allow you to pay off the principal on the loan regularly. Further, a balloon payment coming at the end of the term could create a major financial problem. Though a bank might allow you an extended time to pay, it usually means that less principal is being paid to bring down the loan's balance. Even if the bank allows small payments, it may take years to repay a modest loan.

The cost of applying for a home equity loan may be a deterrent. Closing costs include application fees, appraisal fees, and lawyer fees, possibly even a title search and title insurance—all of which may amount to $1,000 or more.

Use a home equity loan with caution. If you must borrow this way, try to negotiate a time in the future when the home equity loan can be converted to a conventional loan. This will be to your advantage as interest rates on conventional financing have dropped.

Make sure that any disclosure problems that might affect the terms of your loan are written in the loan agreement.

■ *KEY POINT: Negotiate converting your home equity loan to a conventional loan sometime in the future.*

WHY A HOME EQUITY LOAN IS WORTH CONSIDERING

For financing a major expense, such as college tuition or medical bills, the home equity credit line is one way to tap the equity you may have in your home—and keep up to $100,000 interest deductibility.

The interest rate itself is lower on home equity loans than other types of consumer debt such as credit card balances, car loans, and personal loans. With the phaseout of interest deductions for most of these loans, home equity loans are the only type of tax-deductible consumer borrowing except regular home mortgages.

■ *KEY POINT: A home equity loan carries a comparably lower interest rate and is deductible up to $100,000.*

Just as in negotiating other loans with a variable interest rate, it is wise to choose a loan with an interest rate cap so you can afford the payments if the rates rise to that maximum. Further, as with any mortgage borrowing, payments should not exceed one-third of your before-tax income.

■ *KEY POINT: As with any mortgage loan, keep payments within one-third of your budget.*

A home equity loan is an excellent way to borrow without refinancing your first mortgage. It is like a second mortgage, only more flexible. You don't need to take the money until you actually need it, so you don't pay the interest until you put the money to use.

The competition among banks for these loans is extensive, and many banks don't go through the full mortgage process such as appraisal, credit check, and legal fees if they are particularly anxious to give the loan.

■ *KEY POINT:*   *Competition between banks keeps down the cost of services.*

The best possible bank to turn to is usually the one that already holds your first mortgage. You can verify this assumption when you talk to lenders about waiving many of the closing costs.

■ *KEY POINT:*   *The bank to approach is the one that holds your present mortgage.*

Banks are very competitive on these loans because they benefit from them; you in turn can benefit by gaining a bank's quick decision on your application. By providing the proper information, you can usually secure a commitment within 24 hours.

■ *KEY POINT:*   *Banks are often motivated to make rapid decisions.*

With the home equity loan, you can take the full amount of the money immediately, as you would on a second mortgage. Or you can take it as you need it by using a check or, with special arrangements, a credit card. Refinancing and second loans can usually run 5 to 15 years; home equity loans often run longer and can even be open-ended.

This is an excellent way to finance major expenses such as education or medical needs, as long as you are aware of the problems. First, you want to reduce closing costs, as these fees must be paid up front. Second, realize that you have put your house up for security as collateral, which can be a risk if you are unable to make payments. The interest might vary. You don't want the bank to come after your house.

Finally, certain items such as cars are not good to buy with the home equity line of credit, since the pay-back period for a home equity loan is usually longer than that for a car loan. At the end of a few years, you could have an unpaid balance for the car of more money than it is worth. A normal car loan is paid off in three or four years, approximating the declining value of the vehicle.

■ *CAUTION NOTE: Only finance purchases of significant need or value.*

A home equity loan is one of the major ways you can get at your accumulated equity without selling your house, refinancing it, or taking out a second mortgage. You can simply get a line of credit for the amount of value over your first mortgage that you have in your home. It usually costs less than refinancing and takes less time.

Chapter 13 will discuss the benefits of refinancing your present home.

REFINANCING YOUR EXISTING LOAN

13

In this chapter, we consider the refinancing of an existing loan, perhaps with the gain of additional funds through the transaction.

SAVING MONEY THROUGH REFINANCING

Millions of people who bought homes between 1986 and the present are benefiting from modest interest rates (at least compared with mortgage rates of the preceding 20 years). On the other hand, many people who obtained mortgages between 1978 and 1985 are burdened with high rates, often at double-digit levels.

If you have a mortgage at one of these high rates, you have a fine opportunity to replace it with one at a lower rate, allowing you to save money.

■ *KEY POINT: Today's modest rates offer an opportunity to refinance high-interest mortgages.*

When the rates were high, we had no choice but to negotiate at whatever rate was available. The advantage of owning a property far outweighed the few extra points we had to pay for interest. In addition to a place to live and its attendant tax advantages, ownership meant appreciation. This is a financial advantage over renting that far outweighs a higher interest rate on a mortgage.

225

■ *KEY POINT: The benefits of appreciation, as well as the need for dwelling space and tax advantages, can outweigh the drawbacks of a high-interest mortgage.*

If the restructured mortgage is simply for the remaining principal balance, running the same number of years but with a lower interest rate, it will reduce your monthly mortgage payment and save you thousands of dollars in interest over the life of the mortgage.

You may even wish to stretch out the term of your loan to keep the mortgage payments low. Even if you can afford higher monthly payments, you can negotiate your refinancing for a shorter period, such as 15 years instead of 25, to get the loan paid off as soon as possible.

■ *KEY POINT: Restructuring can gain a lower rate or change the payment term.*

WHEN RENEGOTIATING IS TO YOUR ADVANTAGE

You may already have financing on your properties, and the terms on which you started these loans may be very favorable, both in interest rate and monthly payments. If you negotiated the loan when interest rates were high, however, you may very well want to consider renegotiating both payments and rate. You may even reconsider the amount of time before the loan is paid off. If you don't negotiate the lowest possible deal, you may be paying thousands of extra dollars more than necessary.

■ *CAUTION NOTE: Staying with a high-interest loan is very expensive over time.*

Renegotiating an existing loan is not a difficult process. Usually, if you've had the loan for several years, the principal amount of the loan has diminished and the value of the property has increased. This makes the proportional share of equity to loan amount very favorable and secure. From the bank's point of view, you are an excellent candidate for a restructured loan, and they may even allow you to borrow some more money if you desire.

■ *KEY POINT: Lowered principal balance and higher value are the basis for restructuring.*

Banks don't usually go looking for these loans. Unless a lender can get a higher interest rate, which, obviously, on an existing loan you are not going to agree to, you are not going to be solicited for refinancing. Lenders want to sell new loans at the highest possible rate.

■ *CAUTION NOTE: In times of lower rates, banks don't ask for the business of restructuring loans.*

In restructuring a loan, all your interest costs may not be deductible under the new tax reform laws. Always check with your accountant about any problem that could occur with refinancing.

TARGETING THE LEAST EXPENSIVE MONEY

Normally, the first mortgage, whether an original loan or a refinancing, is the cheapest money you can borrow. Anything else—commercial loans, a second mortgage, or even a home equity loan—costs more in interest rate and has less favorable terms.

■ *KEY POINT: First mortgage interest is often less than that for other types of financing.*

As there are many ways to negotiate first mortgage loans, there are many ways to restructure your existing loan. The most common loan is the monthly amortization with constant monthly payments paid over a set time, normally varying anywhere from 15 to 30 years. By negotiating a lower interest rate

	30-Year Loan	20-Year Loan	15-Year Loan
Principal amount	$ 80,000	$80,000	$80,000
Interest rate	9%	9%	9%
Number of payments	360	240	180
Monthly payment	$644	$720	$811
Overall interest cost	$151,729	$92,748	$66,055
Savings	(base)	$58,981	$85,674

Table 13.1.   Term comparison.

for this type of loan, you will pay less money out in interest over the long term.

If you are financially able, another way to renegotiate your loan is to keep the same interest rate but change the term from 25 or 30 years to 20 or 15 years. As shown in Table 13.1, the savings can be dramatic.

■ *KEY POINT:*   *A lower interest rate or a shorter term can save considerable money.*

As with first mortgages, you can also make more rapid repayments or lump-sum reductions of loans, such as balloon payments, at specific periods or at the end of the loan term.

RENEGOTIATING THE BEST TERMS

When refinancing any loan, negotiate to repay that loan in a bulk amount (such as from a sale of the property) without incurring any points or penalty. Also negotiate a minimal penalty should you need to close the loan out before the end of its term.

■ *KEY POINT:*   *In renegotiating an existing loan, you can often drop any prepayment penalty.*

As just mentioned, if you are not changing the interest rate but simply the term, usually the bank is happy to waive any prepayment penalties.

DISCOUNTING THE LOAN BALANCE

Most people, at the time they sell their property, pay the entire principal balance of their mortgage on that property. Certainly, the lender allows little choice; full payment is required at the time of the closing, and the bank often handles the paperwork to make sure of getting its money.

However, one possibility that you may wish to explore with your bank, although admittedly not one that banks usually favor, is discounting the loan balance. Lenders faced with low interest rates socked in for a long term might very well be willing to discount the principal balance to get back the bulk of their money. This they can lend out at a higher rate.

■ *KEY POINT: Lenders on occasion, discount the principal balance for a long-term, low-interest loan.*

If the reason you are paying off the loan is the sale of your property, your negotiating position with the lender is nil. But is there a specific action that would cause a change in your mortgage? Try logic. You may propose that if the bank will take a discounted payoff in the principal amount due on your loan, they can then reinvest these monies more profitably. Your approach to them might be that you have come into some extra money, perhaps from a family inheritance, and want to pay off the mortgage, but only if discounted.

■ *CAUTION NOTE: If a lender suspects a sale, discounting is not possible.*

Usually, if the loan is profitable, the lender is not interested in discounting. Banks want to close out only those loans that are unprofitable for them, particularly because of a low interest rate or lack of points.

■ *CAUTION NOTE: Profitable loans cannot be discounted.*

You are not likely to get the lender to agree to a large discount; at most you will get 20% or 30%. The lender must relend it at a much better rate than the discounted rate to make money in discounting the payoff to you.

It is helpful in negotiating for you to know the rate of return on alternative investments available to the lender. For example, if you have an old 5% loan and current rates are 9.5%, the bank may allow you some discount to get most of their investment back.

■ *KEY POINT:*   *Knowing alternative rates will help in negotiating a discount with your lender.*

COSTS OF REFINANCING

You need to be concerned with more than just interest rates. Other factors such as points and prepayment penalties need to be considered in a decision about refinancing. The lender may require a termite inspection or other wood-boring insect inspection. These costs can vary between $40 and $60. Often, the lender may want to update the credit report, which costs anywhere from $30 to $45. An application fee may be charged, possibly waived. Follow the advice in Chapter 1 and update much of the information on the property and your own personal financial statements—both crucial to the lender—yourself.

■ *KEY POINT:*   *Many loan charges, although often less than those for starting the original first mortgage, come with refinancing.*

Points are often the largest obstacle to refinancing. The lender may want to charge one or more percentage points of the mortgage amount to make the deal. This amount has to be weighed against what you hope to save.

■ *CAUTION NOTE:*   *Excessive points must be compared with what will be saved.*

Other charges, such as recording fees, also will apply to the new financing. Some banks require title insurance, the cost of which can vary from bank to bank. The title search is often done by the private attorney you hire, who in turn certifies the title of the property to the bank. This fee may be discounted if you are refinancing your loan with the existing bank. At the very least, the lawyer or whoever you had do the title search in the beginning may give you a discount on doing it again.

Be sure to consult your personal attorney if you refinance, to make sure there are no hidden costs and services and that documents are recorded as they should be.

■ *KEY POINT: Always consult your personal attorney when refinancing.*

Refinancing costs are not as steep as the original costs. Restructuring may sound like a simple transaction of exchanging the balance of your existing mortgage for a new loan carrying a lower interest rate. With the same lender, it is less complicated than the original negotiations. With a new lender, however, the costs may be higher.

Doing business with the lender that carries your existing loan allows greater flexibility in discounting the costs of refinancing. For example, a credit check probably is unnecessary if you have a good record of paying your present mortgage. Even so, the same bank is likely to charge points, but often not as many on refinancing as on the original loan.

■ *KEY POINT: Doing business with the same lender usually means fewer closing costs.*

MAKING THE DECISION

Many factors will affect your decision on refinancing a property. One is the burdensome cost of an existing first mortgage combined with a second mortgage or even a consumer loan. You may be better off with a new first mortgage that will encompass these other loans, perhaps going back to the original loan amount or even exceeding it. Even if you use this money to pay other costs besides your existing loan balance on the property, you might be saving interest overall.

■ **KEY POINT:**   *Refinancing can combine several loans and add monies.*

Usually refinancing is more important if you are going to keep your property for a long time. The extra charges involved in restructuring a loan, although not as much as for negotiating the original loan, can bring down your overall savings unless you plan to stay in the property. If you are considering selling in the near future, it may actually pay you to keep going with your current higher rate.

■ **CAUTION NOTE:**   *Costs to close a loan can be excessive unless you hold the property for several years.*

The primary reason you want to renegotiate a loan is to get a lower interest rate than that on your present mortgage. The danger is that the expenses of refinancing may offset its benefits. While refinancing may be easy to get, you should shop around among lenders to see what costs are involved and if the transaction is worthwhile for you.

THE 2-2-2 SOLUTION AND ITS FALLACY

It is difficult to offer a fixed formula for making a refinancing decision, but a good guide to help you decide is called the "2-2-2 solution." Specifically, if the interest rate potentially available to you is 2% less than you are now paying, if you plan to stay in your home for more than 2 years, and if the refinancing charges don't exceed $2,000, refinancing may make sense for you.

■ **KEY POINT:**   *In general, refinance when the potential interest rate is 2% less than your current rate, you plan to stay in the house at least two more years, and the costs are less than $2,000.*

The 2-2-2 solution assumes your mortgage is large enough to make the restructuring good for you. If the interest rate difference is less, you must look more carefully at the refinancing charges and the amount of money that you are gaining in the refinancing. You compare whether you are just paying off an existing loan to get lower payments, or your payments are staying the same but you are gaining back some money, perhaps to the level of original financing or even more.

Use the 2-2-2 solution as a thinking tool to help make the best decision about refinancing, but don't get locked into it as a firm rule. Instead of relying on any special technique, focus on your purpose. Are you refinancing mainly to reduce your monthly payment, or total cost over time? If you want to trim your payment, shop for the lowest rate as well as transaction costs. Then, calculate how long you would have to stay in your house before the total of your monthly savings would offset the closing costs. To do this, divide the dollar amount of monthly savings into the transaction cost to find the number of months until you break even. You must now plan to be in your house longer than this point.

If your aim is to cut interest paid out over time, then you must consider refinancing for a shorter term. Your monthly payments may not be lower, but as you have seen by many examples presented here, you can save tens of thousands of dollars in interest charges. Whether you refinance for short- or long-term savings, you need to decide how long you expect to hold your home, how much you can afford each month, and how much interest you wish to save over time.

■ *KEY POINT: In refinancing, check the overall benefits of a lower rate, future time, and closing costs.*

CALCULATING YOUR SAVINGS

Refinancing must provide you with an economic benefit—you can't give up more than it is worth to gain the extra money. If you are going to be selling your house within a year or two, any small gain may not be worth the difference or the effort. As an example, if you have an $80,000, 25-year mortgage at a fixed rate of 11.5%, your monthly payment is $813. If you refinance the same mortgage at 9.25%, your monthly payment is $685, or a savings of $128 per month. If your refinancing costs are $3,000, it will take you almost 24 months to recoup these charges before you begin to see any real savings on your mortgage. If you are staying longer than two years in your property, then refinancing makes sense.

■ *KEY POINT:* *Savings are gained only after recouping closing costs.*

A further example: If you now have a 30-year, $65,000 mortgage with a fixed rate of 11.5%, you can refinance with a 20-year loan at 8.5%. This assumes your refinancing costs are modest and you will be in your home for at least 4 or 5 years. This extra 3% difference in interest makes the restructuring worthwhile, because at 11.5% you are paying $644 each month. And, by refinancing at 8.5% you are paying $500, a savings of $144 per month. If your refinancing charges amount to $2,600, you will recover that cost within 18 months.

What you also must compare is the helpful aspect of paying the loan off in a shorter time. Again, part of the key is staying in the property beyond the time it takes to pay your refinancing charges. Additionally, you will be putting yourself into a payment plan that will pay less interest.

For example, assume you have a 30-year, 11.5% fixed-rate mortgage of $55,000, which you can refinance for 20 years at 9.75%. You are presently paying $545 monthly. After refinancing, your monthly costs will be $522, a savings of only $23. Assuming refinancing charges of $3,500, it will take you more years than the mortgage will run to regain this closing money. However, the kicker is that you will be paying only half as much in interest—$70,206 instead of $141,077—a $70,871 savings.

As in the previous example, you are paying off your loan in 20 years under the new refinancing rather than the original 30 years. This may sound helpful, but you must remember that you can almost always pay a mortgage more rapidly than required. In the previous example, the monthly payments were close to $144 lower per month; here they are similar enough to make the decision to restructure dependent on the value of paying off the loan earlier.

■ *KEY POINT:*   *In deciding to refinance, compare monthly savings and any change of term against paying off closing costs.*

If you have taken out an adjustable-rate loan, the situation is similar. Let's assume that you have a $75,000, 25-year ARM; in the beginning, the rate was 11%, but it has now declined to 7.5% because of a general lowering. Your potential new loan is a fixed-rate mortgage at 8.75%. The question is, is it worth it to refinance? You are not going to see a significant difference in monthly payments, and it will take a long time to recover your refinancing charges. However, since at some time in the future, interest rates on your adjustable-rate mortgage are likely to rise again, boosting your present monthly cost, it might be wise for you to go for the lower fixed-rate mortgage to assure yourself against any future rise.

When you started the loan, your ARM at 11% was $735 monthly. Now, it is 7.5% and $554 monthly. Refinancing at the higher conventional rate of 8.75%, you will pay $618 monthly. Here, there is no savings. However, if rates do rise again, which surely they will (historically, they have cycled upward), the fixed-rate mortgage stabilized at 8.75% may be the optimal financial decision for you.

The preceding examples are easy to think through because they don't take into consideration that you have held your existing mortgage for a certain number of years. The following example more realistically compares the costs of refinancing an existing loan with the savings that result from a lower monthly payment. The loss of earned interest on the refinancing cost is also computed.

Let's assume 4 years ago, you financed a home with a 30-year, 11% fixed-rate mortgage for the amount of $110,000. The monthly payments are $1,048, and the loan carries a penalty of 1.5% if the loan balance is paid off within the first 6 years.

Mortgage rates have dropped, and you can refinance the balance of $107,648 for 25 years at 8.75%. The monthly payments will be $885, and the new loan carries a 2% penalty if paid off prematurely.

Refinancing charges include $2,500 in origination and other fees, two points of the new loan amount, and the 1.5% penalty for paying off the existing loan.

Further, each option will be tested by determining the net present value at an average 6% earnings rate of the next 60 payments (assuming you wish to sell in 5 years).

After calculations (an inexpensive financial investment calculator will make quick work of your specific situation), considering the 6% earnings rate and the refinancing charges, the net present value of the new loan is $106,945. This is much less than the $131,134 net present value for the existing loan, so the refinancing option is favorable.

ALTERNATIVE MORTGAGE PLANS

The most widespread alternative mortgage is the 15-year fixed-rate. If you can keep payments the same—if refinancing from a 30-year mortgage at 10% to 12%, for example—you can pay off the loan in half the time. When providing for retirement or sending youngsters to college, it would be advantageous to be out from under mortgage payments. As demonstrated in other examples in this book, huge savings in total interest result from paying off a loan in 15 years rather than 30 years.

■ *KEY POINT: Refinancing from a term of 30 years to 15 years saves considerable interest.*

The only doleful aspect to dropping to a 15-year mortgage is you will lose a measure of tax deductibility on interest paid as well as tie up more of your money than if you swapped for a lower-rate 30-year fixed loan. It is true that if you put the difference in money you would pay on a 30-year loan compared with a 15-year loan in the bank each month you would come out ahead. The idea is that with this extra money you could pay off the loan in 15 to 20 years, while along the way, you would have a bigger tax break as well as excess cash in case of emergency.

An additional way to beat the odds on paying off a long-term mortgage is to make an extra payment of principal each year. This means you will finish a 30-year loan in about 20 years.

■ *CAUTION NOTE:* *You lose deductibility and tie up cash in a 15-year loan.*

■ *KEY POINT:* *Banking the payment difference or making an annual extra principal payment is the best strategy for continuing a long-term mortgage.*

Mastering either of the latter two strategies provides a method for self-refinancing. If you don't feel that over time you can maintain such a self-disciplined program, consider the 15-year refinancing plan with its mandated payments.

Use the worksheet shown in Figure 13.1 to help you compute different refinancing plans.

THE BEST SOURCE FOR YOUR REFINANCING NEEDS

Although you should investigate the interest rates and terms of all local lenders, the best place to start negotiating is the lender of your first mortgage.

As you can judge, one of the biggest obstacles to refinancing is the amount of fees and charges you will have to pay. Jumping down from a 13% to a 10% interest may look good on paper, but if you have to spend $4,000 just to make it happen, it may not be worth it. Your present banker affords you the best opportunity for negotiating lower charges, both on points and matters of title insurance, credit, and appraisal checks.

It's possible your current lender will reduce the present interest rate. This alternative could save much from the cost of a conventional refinancing. Changing an existing loan to a lower rate involves much less work than processing a complete

Refinancing Cost

    Application fee $_____

    Appraisal   _____

    Survey   _____

    Credit report   _____

    Title search   _____

    Title insurance   _____

    Inspections   _____

    Underwriting fee   _____

    Recording fees   _____

    Lawyer's fee   _____

    Miscellaneous costs   _____

Total Cost of Refinancing $_____

Computation of Payback Time

    a. Current monthly payment $_____
       (principal & interest)

    b. New monthly payment   _____
       (Subtract)

    c. Before-tax savings   _____
       (per month)

    d. Marginal tax bracket   _____
       (Multiply and subtract)

    e. After-tax savings   _____
       (per month)

    f. Number of months to break even   _____
       (Divide monthly savings into total
       cost of refinancing)

Figure 13.1.   Refinancing worksheet.

refinancing. Your bank may be willing to keep valued customers from taking their business elsewhere.

In a conventional refinancing, your present lender may charge you some points to begin the refinanced loan, but may forgive any prepayment charges that exist in your present mortgage contract. If you go to a new bank, you are going to have to face prepayment penalty points charged by your old lender, as well as the points charged by your new lender. If you are charged more than three points, refinancing may not be profitable for you.

Your present lender knows that you are serious about paying off your old mortgage. You are bound to gain a most helpful refinancing deal, perhaps requiring only a point or two instead of the more average three to four points.

■ *KEY POINT: Start refinancing negotiations with your present lender.*

Even if your bank has sold your mortgage in the secondary market, it will continue to service the loan by collecting the payments, earning an annual servicing fee of about 0.25% to 0.50% of the total amount of the loan. If you refinance elsewhere you will be paying off this loan and the original lender will lose this fee, so this lender is most likely to offer you a competitive deal to keep your business.

USING A SECOND MORTGAGE TO RESTRUCTURE YOUR EXISTING FINANCING

You should always consider second mortgage loans in restructuring the financing of your home. There are, however, several attendant dangers. One is that interest rates on a second mortgage are usually not favorable—often they are some of the highest rates consumers can pay. Second, they can add considerably to the amount of your monthly payments. Not only do you have your existing first loan payments, but you have a second mortgage payment that is secured by your house.

■ *CAUTION NOTE: Rates and overall payments on second mortgages are higher than those on other forms of financial restructuring.*

As with home equity credit lines, banks are always anxious to lend money in the form of a second mortgage; so, it is easy to negotiate with them in less than a day's time.

Unfortunately, with a second mortgage, the bank often isn't concerned about assets and balance sheet or verifying your income. Rarely will they even run a credit check. What they are concerned about is the amount of equity or the difference between the value of your property and the principal balance on your first mortgage loan. They are making the loan on the basis of your equity rather than on your ability to pay. Payments can be difficult for those whose income may vary because of the nature of their work. Foreclosure is an ever-present risk in negotiating any second mortgage, which makes it a much higher risk than renegotiating your existing first loan.

■ *CAUTION NOTE: Be cautious when you are the only judge of your ability to pay.*

Although sometimes the mortgage can be speedily negotiated, this may not be best for you. You should always make sure you have a wise use for this money, and that your payments and interest rate are not exorbitant or more than you can comfortably handle.

Many borrowers who have become overburdened and find it difficult to make payments discover that the banks with which they originally negotiated their loans no longer hold them. Their loans have been sold along with other loans to groups of investors, who unvaryingly make the decision to foreclose when payments aren't being made. This sort of abuse can lead to much fraud in the lending industry.

The key object in getting a second mortgage is making sure there are no terms in the fine print you do not understand and that haven't been negotiated, and that you can meet all your expenses. You must decide whether this arrangement is better than negotiating additional funds by restructuring your first mortgage loan.

■ *KEY POINT:* *Restructure your first mortgage before considering a second mortgage.*

INTEREST DEDUCTIBILITY IN REFINANCING

Deductibility of mortgage interest in refinancing can fall into two categories: acquisition debt and home equity debt. Acquisition debt is incurred by refinancing your old mortgage up to the amount of the refinanced debt. Often, home equity debt is money not used to purchase or to improve property. Your single refinancing, then, can be both acquisition debt and home equity debt.

For example, if you gain more money refinancing your present mortgage balance by using part of the refinancing proceeds to pay off your original mortgage and the rest to pay off a personal debt, even though this is all one loan, it qualifies partially as acquisition indebtedness and partially as home equity indebtedness. The interest on the home equity portion of the new refinancing loan is fully deductible as long as the debt does not equal the lesser of the fair market value of your home minus the total acquisition debt, or $100,000 ($50,000 if you're married and file separate returns). Even if you own two homes, the upper limit on your home equity debt, whether on one or both homes, still may not exceed $100,000.

■ *KEY POINT:* *Interest on refinancing is deductible up to $100,000.*

You give up deductible interest by refinancing at lower rates. For example, if you are in the 38% combined federal and state marginal tax bracket and took out a $100,000, 30-year loan two years ago at 10.5%, you would at this point have paid off little principal. By contemplating a new loan at 8.5% accompanied by points and fees of $4,000, your total borrowing will be $104,000. Although you will be paying 2% less in interest, saving $115 per month, the reduction in deductible interest means that you will have paid $2,099 more in taxes four years from now than you would have if you didn't refinance. In fact, the savings from your new loan won't come until the 50th month. Excluding taxes, savings would have come after month 38.

■ *CAUTION NOTE: Losing deductibility may cause high-income taxpayers to wait longer for savings in refinancing.*

The worksheet shown in Figure 13.2, can help you make a refinancing decision based on tax savings. Calculations on this worksheet are based on refinancing with a mortgage of similar length.

You need to use caution if you qualify for the new alternative minimum tax (AMT), a flat tax of 21% for those whose legitimate deductions reduce the regular tax they owe below the

---

a. Length of remaining time
   (Multiply by years to get months)   _____

b. Monthly savings between loans
   (Multiply)   _____

c. Higher amount you would pay in income
   taxes with lower-rate mortgage
   (Subtract)   _____

d. Estimated closing costs
   (Subtract)   _____

e. Prepayment penalty on present loan
   (Subtract)   _____

f. Savings/loss $_____
   (Estimated)

Figure 13.2.   Refinancing savings.

amount their income suggests. There are limits on the deductibility of a refinanced mortgage for AMT purposes. A quick way to determine what is deductible under AMT is to divide your old mortgage balance by the total amount of your new loan. The result is the deductible percentage of interest on your refinanced mortgage. As with any tax computation, check with your accountant on any changes in the tax law.

FIVE GUIDELINES FOR REFINANCING

1. Lock in a favorable interest rate. Do what you can even if it means paying a point or two extra to negotiate the lowest interest rate.

2. Only refinance for as much money as you need. Refinancing your property, as seen in the discussion on home equity loans, can be an excellent way to gain money for your child's college tuition or for some essential remodeling. It is not the way to buy a car, a boat, or any other large depreciable item, or to take an expensive vacation. You are pledging your home as security for the loan, so negotiate the lowest possible charges. The interest rate difference may be very attractive, but if the charges and fees to get this loan are too high, it can take you years to achieve any true savings on refinancing.

3. Avoid prepayment penalties, if possible. If you need to sell soon or at any time while your loan is still in existence, you shouldn't be charged for paying your loan before the end of its term. If you cannot avoid a prepayment penalty, make sure that it is a percentage based on the future balance of the loan, not on the original amount.

4. Don't refinance if you plan to move within two to three years. The charges needed to make this loan often destroy any savings, unless you plan to remain with the loan, hence the property, for a four- or five-year period. Make sure in refinancing that you're going to stay put for a while.

5. Refinance to a shorter payment schedule. This may add little to your monthly payment, but it can save in overall interest paid. An alternative is to add principal payments on a regular basis or to pay biweekly, thereby pruning 7 years and 8 months off a 30-year loan. These are all options that will save tens of thousands of dollars in interest cost.

Chapter 14, the final chapter, shows how to structure superior mortgages in trading up or down.

USING LOW RATES TO TRADE UP OR DOWN

Recent low rates allow present homeowners, for the same amount of money, to consider buying a larger home with more amenities. Or, a smaller one with less maintenance while saving more for other expenses.

Lower rates also allow new buyers to increase their price ranges. If all you could afford last year was a run-down older house, this year a newer home with amenities may be in the offing.

■ *KEY POINT: Low interest rates enhance trading up or down.*

Although low rates seldom combine with low prices, this phenomenon is apparently related to our coming out of a minirecession. In many areas of the country, real estate has been crippled. National economic considerations, however, have conspired to bring both rates and prices in line with the rising expectations of many buyers.

LOW RATES INCREASE AFFORDABILITY

A lower rate permits you to pay a little more—to be at the upper end of a price range rather than fishing for the right home at the low end. Extra money that might be going to satisfy a higher rate mortgage can now be used to increase the amount of the mortgage. Hence, it increases the amount you can afford to pay for the house.

For example, an interest rate differential of 2% can make a real difference. If you started looking for a house when interest rates were 9.75%, and by the time you were ready to close, the rate had dropped to 7.75%, your payments for a $75,000 loan for 20 years would be $616 instead of $711. This is a real savings of $95 per month. At the 7.75% rate, this monthly $95 permits you to afford an additional $11,572 in mortgage value. A lower rate, then, provides greater purchasing power.

■ *KEY POINT:*   *Low rates make more house affordable.*

Affordable interest rates are not only for first-time buyers—they also are beneficial to you in buying another house—trading up or down. If you already have your starter, or second or third, home, you may now want to get a little more space or more luxury. Or, you may want to downsize as the children leave.

TRADING UP—LARGER AND FANCIER

You may already have lived comfortably in a starter house you bought 8 to 10 years ago. You have had several additions to your family and feel you would like more space. Much to your delight, you find that the five-bedroom, three-and-a-half–bath contemporary with tennis court next to the apple orchard in a better neighborhood is available at a fraction of what it would have cost a few years ago. Your income has increased, adding funds to what you could pay on a mortgage each month.

The mortgage on your present house is $750 per month, based on a $130,000 loan at 10.5% paid back through 25 years. Your original purchase price was $162,500, which has increased modestly to $190,000. Your mortgage balance after 8 years is $103,870. The new dream house, which at one time might have sold for close to a half million, now can be bought for $325,000. After transaction costs, you have $78,000 equity to put up as a down payment. This is 24% of the new purchase price, leaving a balance of $247,000. Financed at 7% over 25 years, your new payments would be $1,200 per month. If you could muster some additional funds as a down payment, your monthly cost would be lower.

■ *KEY POINT:* *Less interest cost can propel you into a larger house.*

What you are doing is paying an additional $450 per month over your present $750 to gain a new home that is worth almost twice as much as your present home. Although its increased value is important, your primary motivation is the increased utility (not to mention pleasure) of the new residence for you and your family.

■ *CAUTION NOTE:* *Higher monthly cost must translate into more utility and service.*

If rates had remained at 10.5%, the monthly payment would be $1,422. Or, almost double your present payment. Total interest paid over the 25 years at 10.5% would be $180,000. At 7%, it is a still hefty but more modest $113,000.

TRADING UP WHEN YOU CANNOT GET AS MUCH FOR YOUR PRESENT HOUSE

When trading up in some markets, you cannot get as much money for the same property as would have been possible several years ago. Although you must sell at a loss, you can get a bargain buying up the ladder. Although you get less for your present house, a larger and more amenity-filled (read more expensive) home is offered at a greater discount.

For example, with interest rates helping out, you decide to sell your present two-bedroom home. Five years ago, you paid $150,000; now you can only get $135,000—a $15,000 loss. This amount is more if you consider that what you do with money is supposed to increase in value over time. However, you put market conditions to work by trading up for a larger, nominally more expensive house. Your new dream house, a five-bedroom larger house originally listed at $210,000, now at $180,000 gives you a $30,000 savings. You more than make up for what you lose on your present house.

■ *KEY POINT:*   *A loss in selling your present house is more than made up when buying a larger, more expensive home.*

The asking price of the new house would have been somewhat higher several years ago, just as yours was. However, the difference is likely to have been proportionally greater because the prices of expensive homes are more volatile; that is, they fluctuate more than prices for moderate homes.

You have saved $15,000, possibly more. Though you don't get as much for your property, you still benefit by jumping up in size and quality.

And, as in the previous example, you also benefit by a lower interest rate.

TRADING DOWN—SMALLER AND COZIER

As common as buying a larger house to fill with a growing family is seeking a smaller house as the need for space lessens. Typically, once the children are grown or off at school, the need for the four- or five-bedroom megahome changes. A two- or three-bedroom dwelling will suffice—perhaps even a duplex or townhouse, with less maintenance than the free-standing house required.

Often there's an extended dollar saving in trading down. It's not unusual to sell a large five-bedroom home in the $250,000 price range. This may net $50,000 to $100,000 when you purchase a smaller home at $150,000 to $200,000.

■ *KEY POINT:*   *Trading down can fit reduced size needs as well as producing extra cash.*

Another way to look at the savings you gain by trading down is that for every $10,000 you gain in lower house cost, you will have $87 dollars a month (at 8.5% interest rate) for other expenses.

Let's imagine your present spacious home has more than met the needs of you and your now grown family. With children leaving the nest, taking care of the pool has become a chore. Two of the extra bedrooms have been taken over by storage. Even the extra garage bay has turned into a place for clutter. You and your spouse have started to think about moving to smaller quarters with less upkeep.

You only have a $20,000 balance on your present mortgage. You understand from your local real estate broker your house would sell for $165,000. After transaction costs, you would have almost $140,000. You find your new dream house—two bedrooms, no pool, in wooded setting—for the bargain price of $125,000. After consultation with your accountant, you decide not to pay all cash but put down only $90,000 of the $140,000. You keep $50,000 for other investments and to satisfy a potential tax.

Since you are buying down (assuming you are not yet 55 years of age where you qualify for a one-time $125,000 deduction) you will have to settle taxes for the difference in values. Again, with your accountant, you calculate your old tax basis (cost plus improvements) and how it fits into your new property. Since your new purchase price is not far from the purchase price of your original house, most of your tax basis can be transferred into the new property, lessening your overall tax.

■ *CAUTION NOTE: Trading down may trigger tax consequence.*

You have, then, a more suitable home requiring less maintenance with extra cash left over.

BARGAIN WITH BUILDERS WHEN TRADING UP OR DOWN

New home deals abound. Although waiting lists are beginning to build for medium-price homes, there are still many bargains.

Often recession-battered buyers have had to walk away from their deals, and builders have been forced to sell at a loss. For example, a house that may have originally been offered at $175,000 to $250,000, now may be offered for as much as $45,000 to $85,000 less.

■ *KEY POINT:* *Benefit by a builder's need to sell at a loss.*

As the housing boom sputters and jerks forward, many builders get caught with expensive land. This is especially true for small and medium-size contracting firms without the financial resources to sustain cost. Stacks of debts to lenders, suppliers, and subcontractors pile up because many houses are left unsold. Builders are then forced to sell off their excess inventory at any cost to keep their companies viable. Big discounts can result, particularly in areas where the housing market heated quickly and then died from having been overbuilt: New England, California, metropolitan New York, Phoenix, Arizona, and Washington, D.C. In the Midwest and South where there was less overbuilding, discounting is not as strong. In all areas, however, there are plentiful opportunities to buy from individual builders who have overbuilt.

These buying opportunities are not likely to remain for long. When the housing market becomes more active, inventories shrink. Prices then rise. Often, the best financial deals are made early.

■ *CAUTION NOTE:* *Buy while bargains abound—before the market takes off.*

STRETCH ONLY IF NECESSARY

Stretch your resources as long as you don't spread yourself too thin. Back in the late 1970s and early 1980s, buyers were often advised to extend to the limit to buy as much house as they could afford. The reasoning behind this approach was that prices were expected to continue a dramatic rise. This advice was wrong for several reasons: (1) Buyers gained more space than they needed; (2) budgets became strained as utility bills increased; (3) real estate values went on a downslide, remaining stable only in a few areas.

Therefore, you should digest only as much property as you can swallow.

■ *CAUTION NOTE:* *Prices fall as well as rise.*

Today, you don't want any more space than you need to satisfy your living needs. Further, with energy costs high, you don't need extra space to heat and cool. Home prices are not predicted to increase to the same degree or as fast as they did in the past. Modest growth is the watchword, and then only if the property is wisely bought in the beginning. Prices will rise, just not as dramatically as before.

■ *CAUTION NOTE:* *Don't buy more house than you need.*

As a homeowner, you don't want every last dollar of income going to mortgage payments. You have many other expenses. Extend yourself only if you need the features, such as space, style, and location, provided by the house you want to buy—and if you are confident that you will stay put for the near future.

The lesson is, don't extend yourself unless you know your income will increase to ease the burden of higher payments.

SELLING A PRICEY HOME

If you own an expensive home, or at least a home that is in the upper range of value in your area, you may have to hold tight awhile. In many markets, pricey homes are behind the sales of low- and middle-range homes.

■ *CAUTION NOTE:* *Higher values lag for expensive homes.*

Be assured that change in the housing market is inevitable. A fair price for your home may be just around the corner. In a few months, maybe just weeks, sales may take off. Even if getting your asking price appears remote now, have confidence. There are many others who share your dilemma.

■ *KEY POINT: Inescapable change will likely skyrocket the value of your present home.*

It hasn't been as much of a seller's market for pricey homes as it has been for less expensive properties. However, sales will pick up in the price range of elite homes. Well-heeled buyers will lose their timidity. The desire to luxuriate in special amenities, gain more space, or enjoy a superior location will always tempt those who have built up equity in modest houses. Although it takes longer for them to comb the market, they will decide at the right time. Therefore, if you wish to downsize and presently own a pricey home, hold fast. A fair offer may come sooner than you expect.

■ *KEY POINT: Be patient in selling an elegant home.*

AT TODAY'S PRICES, DON'T WAIT

In the past few years, the media have had bad news on the housing and mortgage industry: the savings and loan crisis, banks going bust, builders who are bankrupt. How do we as consumers fit into this quagmire? Maybe not so badly: These problems, as well as what may be called the natural economic cycles, have conspired to lower interest rates and keep property values within a larger range of buyers. In many ways, greater real estate opportunities may be available than has been the case in years.

■ *KEY POINT: Benefit from contrary overreaction in the housing market.*

If your dream is to move to a more spacious, newer house, nearer to your children's school, perhaps you should wait no longer. Mortgage interest rates have reached a low. And, although they are likely to remain low for several years, they may have modest rises and falls; you should take timely action. Rates are very likely to be higher by the mid-1990s.

■ *KEY POINT:*   *Low rates promote trade up or down for the right deal.*

While you may be unsure whether you want to make a change now, you might start looking. Even if you don't pre-qualify yourself at the bank because you want to first make certain you want to move in the direction of buying, it doesn't hurt to look at what's on hand. That special house might just be available at a price you could afford.

For example, let's assume 6 years ago you bought a ranch house with three bedrooms and one and a half baths. You negotiated a good interest rate at the time of 10.75%. Your mortgage of $100,000 began at 80% of your purchase price $125,000. After 5 years, the monthly payments of $962 on your 25-year mortgage have brought your principal balance down to $94,766. Your local real estate agent has assured you that because you bought well in a good neighborhood your house has enjoyed a modest appreciation in value. You can probably net, after selling costs, an additional $20,000 more than you originally paid. Although not as dramatic a gain as you might have enjoyed in previous years, it's a modest advance. Your equity is more than $45,000.

With these thoughts in mind, you look to see if a house on the market might offer advantages you don't have in your present house. And, to your pleasant surprise, you find a larger four-bedroom house. It has two full baths, a study, and dining room, and is enhanced with a swimming pool—all for a lower price than you could have afforded when you bought your present house.

■ *KEY POINT:*   *Once you get the buying fever, you might be pleasantly surprised.*

This dream house, which sold 6 years ago for $225,000, now costs only $190,000. Moving your present equity of $45,000 into this house leaves a balance of $145,000, which when mortgaged for a 25-year term at today's comparatively lower rate of 7.5% is $1,072 per month—only $110 a month more than your present payment.

This kind of trade up makes sense only if you feel the amenities of the new house will enhance the lives of you and your family and you can afford the extra, however modest, higher payment. Except, today's lower rate does give you the opportunity to make a deal on more house for the money. Maybe it's a deal you can't pass up.

■ *CAUTION NOTE: Buy only what you can afford.*

A word of caution. Don't procrastinate. Prices of upper-middle and high-end houses will not always be as modest as they are today. Again, we must recognize the principle of change. It's constant. What's true today is not likely to be tomorrow. So, if you're thinking of making a move, even if it's only a dream, give it serious consideration now. You may not have so helpful a pricing structure in the future.

■ *CAUTION NOTE: At this point, don't wait for prices to fall further.*

Even if your present house has not appreciated as much as in the previous example, the dynamics of considering a change now still are true. As we saw before, in trading up you can get a bigger discount on the larger, inherently more expensive house, so it makes sense to deliberate on a possible move. Beyond the near term, as interest rates and values rise, these bargain prices may not hold.

If you are satisfied with your present house and you wish to stay put, reference the chapter on refinancing. There, you will see how to reduce that higher interest rate you started several years ago. Pay particular attention to the formula that charts the additional amount of time you need to stay in a house to make refinancing worthwhile. If you plan to remain where you are for at least two more years, it may make sense to refinance.

■ *KEY POINT: Consider refinancing if you wish to stay put.*

SAVING TAXES WHEN TRADING UP

You will hear about the capital gains debate. Does it apply to you? You will probably never pay capital gains taxes on your home. You are most likely to defer any tax by rolling over any gains into the next house. And then the next, until you qualify to exclude from tax $125,000 in profit at age 55 or pass the home on to your children, free of income tax.

■ *KEY POINT: If you are more than 55, you qualify for a one-time $125,000 deduction.*

You defer tax trading up. In trading down, you will have a tax consequence (subject to the preceding option) governed by the relative difference in value. Specifically, you will pay tax on the difference between the higher tax basis (original purchase price plus major improvements) of the house you are selling and cost (new tax basis) of the house you are buying.

■ *CAUTION NOTE: There is a partial tax consequence for trading down.*

If you sell a home that cost you $200,000, to which you added $25,000 for a family room and two-car garage, you have a total cost of $225,000. Since the property is your home and not technically an investment where you must depreciate a portion each year, the full cost is your tax basis.

If you sell this house for a higher amount, $265,000 for example, then in turn buy a house that costs more than $265,000, you will have no tax. You carry this tax basis with you; in effect, it becomes of no importance as your new tax basis is the higher cost of the new house.

■ *KEY POINT: There is no tax when you trade up.*

If you trade down, however, you have a tax consequence. The difference between this $225,000 tax basis and your new selling price of $265,000 is $40,000. Since your new purchase price of $185,000 is less than your selling price, a portion of the $40,000 will have to be computed with on your year-end tax settlement. If a specific rule on capital gains applies, it may lessen your tax. Consult your accountant.

Sometimes trading up means finding a larger house at less cost than your present one. Depending on where you need to locate, you may find it takes less money to buy more in size, amenities, or location. If you now live in an economically healthy area, where prices have remained high, or at least have rebounded, you may find you can get more for the dollar in another area in which you need to move. It's not uncommon to sell a nice four-bedroom in a large suburban area and, depending on your need, secure a finer five-bedroom home with special amenities for less money, simply by moving to a less populous location.

MASTERING BUYING AND SELLING SIMULTANEOUSLY

Trading up or down requires you to unravel the mysteries of both buying and selling strategies. For starters, you probably cannot tack much on to recent sales prices in your neighborhood. The strategy of setting the price high to leave room to negotiate may send buyers down the road. You can only add on 3% to 5% above the average of recent comparable sales.

■ *KEY POINT: In offering your property for sale, only add modestly to adjusted comparable selling prices.*

You can also avoid offering to help with financing or closing costs. In today's market, however, you must be prepared to vacate fast. Further, if you are selling and the market conditions are conducive, you can get full price, but only if fairly offered. You may command an offer that is free of contingencies, perhaps even from a buyer who has a letter of prequalification.

FIXING UP OR FULL FACE-LIFT

Whether trading up or down in today's market, be prepared to extend yourself. Specifically, make sure your house is competitively offered in price. Additionally, assure its superb appearance.

Price is basically set by the market. What you can do to make your house more appealing is in your control. Whatever the price range of your home, it must compete with other comparable offerings. This is true about used as well as new. Look over your house with a critical eye and fix up any imperfections: broken tile, flaking paint, disconnected gutters. You must spruce up or repair anything that might make your house seem inferior to comparable offerings.

■ *KEY POINT: In offering your home for sale, fix obvious details of deferred maintenance.*

While a full replacement of carpeting, wallpaper, and appliances may be in order, you don't need to go overboard. You don't need to add capital improvements. If you want top dollar, however, you need to bring back into good quality what your house originally had. You can be modest on the expenses.

■ *CAUTION NOTE: In fixing up, don't overspend by making capital improvements.*

What you want to do is fetch in the most amount of money as soon as possible without spending a bundle. A good guideline might be no less a ratio than one to three. For example, if you spend $3,500 fixing up, it should have a potential of bringing back $10,000 in selling price. Or, $5,000 should enhance value to $15,000.

This book has shown you how to get practical financing in the least amount of time. What is more important than an instant loan, however, is a carefully thought out financial plan so you can comfortably pay back the mortgage debt in the ensuing years. I hope the information in this book will help you meet that goal.

INDEX